BAKING
SCIENCE

Foolproof Formulas to Create the Best Cakes,
Pies, Cookies, Breads and More

BAKING
SCIENCE

DIKLA LEVY FRANCES
Creator of One Sarcastic Baker

PAGE STREET
PUBLISHING CO.

PAGE STREET
PUBLISHING CO.

First published in 2022 by
Page Street Publishing Co.
27 Congress Street, Suite 1511
Salem, MA 01970
www.pagestreetpublishing.com

Distributed by Macmillan, sales in Canada by The Canadian Manda Group.

26   25   24   23   22   1   2   3   4   5

ISBN-13: 978-1-64567-454-2
ISBN-10: 1-64567-454-1

Library of Congress Control Number: 2021931946

Cover and book design by Meg Baskis for Page Street Publishing Co.
Photography by Dikla Levy Frances

Printed and bound in the United States

To my dad, Daveed Levy. I love you.
To Mannie, Emily and Juliet, the loves of my life,
my dream come true.

CONTENTS

What Is Baking Science? 10

Stabilizers 16

Ingredients That Add Structure in Baking

Tenderizers 41

Ingredients That Create the Ideal Texture in Baking

Temperature 82

The Force That Transforms Ingredients into Baked Goods

Foolproof Formulas 114

The Easy, Scientific Way to Assure Your Baked Goods Succeed

Putting It All Together   161

Use the Science You've Learned to Take Your Baking to the Next Level!

WHAT IS BAKING SCIENCE?

I first discovered the wonderful world of baking science shortly after I started baking. I wanted to create my very own recipes, but I had no idea which ingredients to use, how much and why.

It was then that I purchased my very first copy of *How Baking Works: Exploring the Fundamentals of Baking Science* by Paula Figoni, a wonderful book that not only answered many of my questions but intrigued me enough to ask even more and continue my exploration, which is still ongoing more than a decade later. I'm so excited to share everything I've learned with all of you!

Before we get started, I would like to take a moment and explain what baking science is and what you can expect from this book.

The phrase "baking science" isn't meant to be sophisticated and intimidating, but it's an indication as to the accuracy of the world that is baking.

As bakers, we all come across a situation when someone we just met says, "You bake? Oh my god! For the life of me, I cannot bake; it's too complicated and precise. I can only cook." And while they're correct to say that baking is a complex and precise process, it's not that different from cooking. After all, when we add salt while cooking, we control the amount—or else the food would be too salty.

We don't tend to think about adding salt to our food as a scientific process, but the fact is that the reason salt should be monitored when added to food is science-based, and it's rooted in the size and structure of the salt molecules. Salt's molecules are much, much smaller than most food molecules, so even when we add ½ teaspoon of salt into, for example, 4 cups (2.2 lb) of vegetables, we're adding the same amount (or close to it) of salt molecules in comparison to the number of molecules of our food. Now, how simple is that?

And much like this explanation of salt, baking science takes a closer look into the molecular structure of common ingredients and explores how they behave in different environments and/or with each other. Carbohydrates like flour and sugar, fats like butter and oil and proteins like eggs all have different molecular structures, shapes and properties, which react differently with each other at different temperatures and when combined in different ways.

Understanding the science behind baking is the key to becoming a better baker. In this book, we'll dive deep and learn the structure and behavior of the molecules in our baking ingredients, as well as techniques to control their reactions.

Knowledge of baking science empowers us to use a simple ingredient in many different ways.

In this book, you'll learn more about common baking ingredients and how they interact with each other and in different environments. We'll take a closer look at temperature and how it's the gas pedal for creating baked goods, as well as how to create the ideal formulas for baked goods from cakes to cookies to piecrust and more. Finally, we'll discover how to apply all that you've learned in this book to create the best baked goods you've always wanted to make and now know how to!

You can use this book as you see fit; read it cover to cover or check the index to find some information about a specific ingredient, method or technique. You can even just explore the book, follow along and bake the recipes just for fun, no science included.

Why Is Water the Most Essential (and Underappreciated) Ingredient in Baking?

Baked goods are a complex and delicate structure of flour, eggs, butter, sugar and other ingredients.

Each ingredient has more than just one role in creating this complex web. For example: Eggs stabilize, emulsify, aerate and add flavor, while butter is used to tenderize, aerate and add flavor.

The one thing that's in common for all of the ingredients, and is sometimes overlooked, is the fact that every ingredient provides moisture through its water content. Eggs are 76 percent water, butter is 12 to 14 percent water and even flour is 7 to 14 percent water.

Water is the essence of life, and that's also true in baking. Water is the most essential ingredient in baking, and without it, baking or eating baked goods would not be a very pleasant experience—or even possible.

The role of water in baking goes beyond helping the ingredients to bind and form a structure.

The contributions of water, or any other form of liquid such as milk, heavy cream, coffee, orange juice and even fruit puree, can be viewed as the foundational brick of baking science. Water is the heart of many chemical, biological and even physical reactions, as we can see from the list below and as we continue our journey into this book.

Water adds moisture and the ideal texture.

In baking, liquids are referred to as moisturizers. They add moisture to provide a pleasant texture to our baked goods.

Water helps with leavening.

During baking, water turns into steam that helps leaven our baked goods.

Water also activates the chemical reaction of baking powder, baking soda and acid, as well as the biological reaction of yeast—all of which leaven our baked goods.

Water transforms sugar.

Sugar dissolves in water, turning the sweetener's texture from coarse and sharp to crispy and brittle or moist and smooth.

Water increases viscosity.

Viscosity is the term that's used to describe the consistency of a liquid. When a liquid is thin like water, for example, its molecules flow by each other fast. This type of liquid is considered to have a low viscosity. If a liquid is thick like applesauce, on the other hand, then its molecules don't have much space to run fast or easily pass each other and it's considered to have a high viscosity.

Starches, like cornstarch, potato starch and even flour, absorb and swell when water is added, increasing the viscosity of our dough or batter, and as a result, thicken, stabilize and provide structure to our baked good.

Water creates elasticity.

A strong elastic gluten net can only form with the presence of water. Gluten is the protein found in flour, and when mixed and stirred with water, the small molecules stretch themselves and bind with each other, creating an elastic texture that prevents our baked goods from crumbling and collapsing. Learn more about gluten and its role in baking on page 17.

Water helps hold baked goods together.

Water helps with the process of emulsification (see the Caramelized Banana Blondies on page 24 to learn more). *Emulsification* is when we mix two ingredients that will not mix naturally, like water and fat. When we emulsify, water is the "receiver," meaning we mix the fat into the water. We do that by creating a lot of tiny bubbles that stay in the water with the help of an emulsifier. Sometimes, if we don't have enough water to keep the fat bubbles separated, then the bubbles tend to bind together and break the emulsification. We see it when our mixture is curdled.

Water helps prevent baked goods from burning.

Water absorbs and conducts (passes on) heat. Water molecules absorb heat faster than other substances, and as they do, they increase their mobility due to the increase in energy. As a result, they pass on some of their energy (heat) to the different molecules around them. However, since water's temperature will never increase beyond 212°F (100°C), it's a great way of preventing our baked goods from overheating and burning.

Water incorporates flavor.

Lemon juice, applesauce, coffee, raspberry puree, banana and even sour cream all have a high percentage of water and can all be used as a source of liquid in our baked goods while providing a distinct flavor.

How do we add liquids to our baked goods?

Now that we know why our baked goods need water, let's answer the questions of how much liquid we should use and how we should incorporate it.

How much liquid you need depends on the formula for the recipe you wish to bake and the percentage of water in each of the ingredients. Chapter 4 (page 82) explores tried-and-true formulas for different types of baked goods.

Most recipes' addition of water is within the ingredients. Ingredients such as fruit puree, milk, sour cream and even cream cheese have a high percentage of water.

A simple Google search will tell you the percentage of water of an ingredient.

Let's take for example, cream cheese, like in this Orange Cream Cheese Cake recipe (page 15). The recipe calls for 1 cup (232 g) of cream cheese. The water content of cream cheese is 50 percent to 55 percent water, so we have a total of ½ cup (120 ml) water.

Therefore, in the recipe mentioned above, there's a total of ⅚ cup (200 ml) of liquids— the ½ cup (120 ml) of water from the cream cheese, plus the ⅓ cup (80 ml) of the orange juice.

The water in the cream cheese contributes to the emulsification process of the fat found in the butter and cream cheese. The orange juice is poured into the butter, helping with the binding of the ingredients, as well as providing flavor, additional moisture and developing gluten. Incorporating orange juice as a liquid in our baking also allows us to incorporate flavor.

The sweet dance of flavors coming from the cream cheese and the orange juice is what gives this cake an amazing zesty and creamy flavor. The cream cheese balances the sweetness of the orange juice, which we can taste in every tender, moist and citrusy bite.

ORANGE CREAM CHEESE CAKE

This sweet, creamy and citrusy cake is a great example of all the ways water helps our baking!

YIELD: One 9-inch (23-cm) cake

2⅓ cups (282 g) all-purpose flour

1¼ tsp (6 g) baking powder

¼ tsp baking soda

1 tbsp (7 g) potato starch

¾ cup (170 g) unsalted butter, room temperature

1 cup (232 g) full-fat cream cheese

1½ cups (300 g) granulated sugar

Zest of 1½ medium oranges

4 large eggs

⅓ cup (80 ml) fresh-squeezed orange juice

NOTE

You can also bake this cake in a 9-inch (23-cm) Bundt pan.

Preheat the oven to 325°F (160°C) and grease the bottom of one 9-inch (23-cm) pan and line it with parchment paper.

In a medium bowl, sift the flour, baking powder, baking soda and potato starch. Mix to incorporate. Set aside.

In the bowl of a stand mixer, place the butter and cream cheese. Beat it on low speed for about 1 minute. Place the sugar in a medium bowl and add the orange zest. Using a fork, blend the orange zest into the sugar until well distributed.

Add the sugar mixture into the butter and cream cheese mixture, increase the mixer speed to medium-high and mix until light and fluffy, 4 to 5 minutes. Scrape the bottom and sides of the bowl.

With the mixer on medium-high speed, add the eggs one at a time, waiting for each egg to fully incorporate before adding the next. Scrape the bottom and sides of the bowl. Reduce the mixer speed to medium-low and add the flour mixture in three stages, alternating with the orange juice and starting and ending with the flour mixture.

As soon as you add the last portion of flour, turn the mixer off and use a rubber spatula to fully incorporate the ingredients.

Pour the batter into the prepared pan and bake for 40 to 45 minutes, or until a toothpick inserted into the center of the cake comes out clean.

Remove the cake from the oven and allow it to cool before inverting, 10 to 15 minutes. The cake should be stored covered at room temperature for up to 4 days or frozen for up to 2 months.

STABILIZERS:
Ingredients That Add Structure in Baking

In baking, ingredients can be divided into two categories: stabilizers and tenderizers. This chapter focuses on the stabilizers, also known in the baking world as "structure builders" and "tougheners."

Stabilizers are the ingredients responsible for the stability and structure of our baked goods. They include basic ingredients like flour, eggs and starch.

Stabilizers can be divided into two types: tougheners and driers. While the tougheners are the ingredients that hold the volume and shape of our baked goods, the driers are the ingredients that absorb moisture. A great example of tougheners are eggs and egg whites and the most common drier in the baking world is starch. Starches, like potato starch and cornstarch, are large, complex carbohydrate molecules that are packed close together and have the ability to absorb liquid. Know that an ingredient can be both a toughener and a drier; for example, flour.

There are different types of stabilizer ingredients—bread flour versus cake flour or whole eggs versus egg whites— as well as different methods we can use to incorporate the ingredients. Choosing the right ingredients along with the right method is key for successful baking and achieving the perfect texture.

While the absence of stabilizers in baking might cause our baked goods to crumble and even collapse, too much might give us a tough, unpleasant result. This is where baking science comes into play. It will help us understand what each ingredient is composed of and how it will contribute to our baked goods.

In this chapter, we'll take a closer look and understand the basic makeup of each of these stabilizer ingredients, its role in baking, what the molecular structure is like and how it contributes to the structure of our baked goods.

The Science Behind the Different Types of Flour, and When to Use Them

In the baking world, flour is one of two main ingredients (eggs being the second) that provide structure and toughness to our baked goods. Flours used in baking are harvested and milled from two types of wheat: hard wheat, which has a higher percentage of strong protein, and soft wheat, which has a lower percentage of somewhat weaker protein.

Let's take a closer look at the scientific makeup of flour, common types and some tips for using it effectively:

The main components found in flour are:

Starches (which make up 72–75%)

Protein (which makes up 6–15%)

Water (which makes up 7–14%)

Sugar molecules (which make up 2%)

The amount of each element differs from one type of flour to the next.

The starches make up the majority of flour. They absorb water, swell and thicken the flour, and in addition, can weaken the gluten, depending on the type of wheat and flour.

The protein in the flour is called gluten. It's what gives our baked goods, breads in particular, an elastic structure and a chewy texture. When the flour is dry, the gluten is inactive, but when wet, the gluten molecules change their shape and get closer to each other, creating a tight network that builds the structure in a baked good.

There is a clear correlation between the amount of liquid we add along with the mixing time and the tightness, strength and texture of the gluten. As we mix flour and water, the gluten molecules stretch themselves, kind of like a spring, and attach to each other in two ways: the first one is sticking to the others and creating thicker, stronger bonds and the second one is attaching from one end of a molecule to the end of another molecule, creating a long molecular bond.

Given the right environment of water and mixing time, the gluten molecules stretch easily and maintain their bond. That's why when dough has developed mature gluten, it's elastic and stretches without tearing.

While strong gluten bonds are desired in baking bread, we wish for weak, minimal gluten bonds when baking cakes, cookies and other baked goods. This is why choosing the correct type of flour determines the success of our baked goods. Different flours are harvested and milled from different types of wheat, which provide different strengths of gluten.

The age of the flour also affects how strong the gluten in it is. As flour ages, the contact with oxygen and the air gradually strengthens the proteins, allowing them to react to each other and form an elastic structure. Therefore, freshly milled flour will have a weak protein that will not perform well, so the process of aging is one of the most important steps in flour production.

(continued)

THE SCIENCE BEHIND THE DIFFERENT TYPES OF FLOUR, AND WHEN TO USE THEM (cont.)

The terms bleached and unbleached refer to the method taken to age the flour. Unbleached flour is flour that was aged naturally with time and bleached flour is flour in which different supplements were added for a faster aging process.

Common Types of Flour

All-purpose flour is the most common flour used in baking, with 9.5 to 13 percent protein. In most cases, it's a combination of hard wheat and soft wheat, but that can change depending on the brand.

All-purpose flour can be found bleached or unbleached, and it can be used for baking cakes, cookies, piecrusts and even bread.

Bread flour is milled from hard wheat. Hard wheat has a higher percentage of strong proteins, a.k.a. gluten. Milling hard wheat also results in a coarser texture and a higher percentage of damaged starches, which absorb more liquids but with minimal swelling. This process helps with the development of strong gluten bonds and provides us with the optimal environment for the elastic texture we search for in bread and other pastries.

Bread flour's high percentage of proteins (11 to 13 percent), meaning its ability to form strong gluten bonds, will create a tough, strong elastic structure, which is why it's a great choice when baking bread. See how I've incorporated this baking science information into a formula for a flawlessly dense, tender loaf on page 159. This formula is built around using a ratio of bread flour, 60 percent of water and a long mixing time to help develop a strong gluten structure.

Cake flour is milled from soft wheat, and as mentioned on the previous page, soft wheat has a weak protein (gluten).

With cake flour, a very particular part of the wheat kernel is milled, giving it a brighter color, a finer powder and a protein percentage of only 6 to 8 percent.

Using chlorine dioxide or chlorine gas also bleaches most cake flours we find in stores. This bleaching treatment enforces the starches' ability to absorb water, swell and, in addition, weaken the gluten bonds.

Cake flour is a great option to bake layer cakes and cookies, but it will not make for good breads or pastries, since the gluten isn't strong enough to create a strong structure.

Pastry flour, much like cake flour, is milled from soft wheat, but unlike cake flour, pastry flour is milled into a very fine meal and not from a specific part of the kernel. That's why its protein percentage is higher than cake flour, averaging 7 to 9.5 percent.

By understanding the makeup of different types of flours, we now know which type of flour to use when baking different types of baked goods. Bread flour is a great option when we bake breads or pastries, pastry flour for pie and cake flour for layer cakes (like in the Cookie Butter Layer Cake recipe on page 19).

As you know, when we bake a cake, we wish for a crumbly, tender texture that holds its shape after the cake cools. With layer cakes, we want to bake an even lighter cake with finer crumbs. Otherwise, a slice that's also layered and frosted with buttery frosting might be too dense.

In the Cookie Butter Layer Cake recipe, we use cake flour to create this perfect cake texture. Remember, cake flour contains only a small amount of gluten. This means that the gluten bonds are weak, resulting in a light cake structure that perfectly complements the rich buttery Swiss meringue buttercream. The high percentage of strong starches will absorb much of the liquid and swell, giving us a high and moist cake (see starch on page 33).

This Cookie Butter Layer Cake is the perfect way to celebrate any special occasion. It's tender, soft, crumbly and full of the warm and comforting flavor of speculoos cookies. Even though one slice is composed of three layers of cake filled with silky smooth Swiss meringue buttercream, the cake is so light and delicious, chances are you'll ask for more.

NOTE

Since flour is powder and it's packed very tightly, it's very important to use a kitchen scale when measuring it. Using a measuring cup is a very convenient option, but the amount of flour packed in 1 cup can vary from 90 grams per cup to 180 grams, and if we use more or less than what the recipe calls for, we might end up with unpleasant results.

COOKIE BUTTER LAYER CAKE

In this recipe, we use our understanding of the scientific makeup of flour, and cake flour in particular, to create the perfect cake texture!

YIELD: One 8-inch (20-cm) cake

CAKE

3⅔ cups (458 g) cake flour

2½ tsp (11 g) baking powder

2½ cups (500 g) granulated sugar

1½ cups (150 g) speculoos cookie crumbs (about 18 cookies)

1½ cups (360 ml) milk, room temperature

½ cup (120 ml) vegetable oil

2 tsp (10 ml) vanilla extract

6 large eggs, room temperature

6 tbsp (120 g) cookie butter

1½ cups (341 g) unsalted butter, room temperature (cut into ½-inch [1.3-cm] pieces)

COOKIE BUTTER SWISS MERINGUE

1 cup (200 g) granulated sugar

½ tsp cream of tartar

6 large egg whites

2 cups (454 g) unsalted butter, room temperature (cut into ½-inch [1.3-cm] pieces)

⅓ cup (100 g) cookie butter

SIMPLE SYRUP

1 cup (240 ml) milk

½ cup (120 ml) water

1 cup (200 g) granulated sugar

(continued)

COOKIE BUTTER LAYER CAKE (cont.)

Preheat the oven to 350°F (175°C). Grease and line the bottom of three 8-inch (20-cm) round pans. Set aside.

In the bowl of a stand mixer fitted with the paddle attachment, sift together the flour, baking powder, sugar and cookie crumbs. Then, beat for 1 minute on low speed to fully incorporate the ingredients.

In a large measuring cup, measure the milk, vegetable oil and vanilla, then add the eggs and cookie butter and whisk with a fork until smooth.

Add the butter pieces to the dry ingredients and beat on medium-low speed, until the butter has been cut into the flour mixture and the mixture resembles a coarse meal, 1 to 2 minutes. Increase the mixer speed to medium-high and pour in the milk mixture. Beat until fully incorporated and smooth, 30 to 60 seconds.

Divide the batter between the three greased pans and bake for 30 to 35 minutes, or until a toothpick inserted into the center of the cakes comes out clean. Remove the cakes from the oven and allow them to cool completely before layering and frosting.

To make the cookie butter Swiss meringue, in the bowl of a stand mixer, mix the sugar and cream of tartar together. Then, mix in the egg whites. Place the bowl on top of a large pan filled with 1 inch (2.5 cm) of simmering water. The water should not touch the bottom of the bowl.

Use a hand mixer to mix the sugar, cream of tartar and egg whites together until the mixture reaches 130°F (55°C) or the sugar has dissolved and you no longer feel its texture when rubbing the mixture between your fingers.

Place the mixing bowl back in the stand mixer and whip on medium-high speed until a stiff meringue has formed. Add the butter one piece at a time. Once the butter is fully added, add the cookie butter and mix until it's smooth and thick.

To assemble, make the simple syrup: In a medium saucepan over high heat, bring the milk, water and sugar to a boil; reduce the heat to medium and cook the mixture for an additional 1 minute, or until the sugar has dissolved and the syrup is smooth.

Place one layer of cake on top of a serving dish. Use a serrated knife to level the top of the cake, then use a pastry brush to soak the first layer with ½ cup (120 ml) of the simple syrup, then spread ⅓ cup (93 g) of the meringue onto the cake. Repeat this process with the remaining two layers, then frost the cake on the top and sides.

The cake should be served at room temperature and can be kept covered for up to 3 days.

Once the cake is frosted, you can drizzle it with some warm cookie butter if desired (make sure it is not too warm or it will melt the frosting). Top with some crushed speculoos cookies to make the cake extra fancy!

How Eggs Build Your Baked Goods' Structure

It's with good reason that whenever we think about baking, eggs are one of the most common ingredients we think of. Eggs are a great provider of structure, and because of that, our baked goods can hold their shape, like a beautiful pound cake or even a cookie. Eggs also provide flavor, a source of fat and can be used in the aeration process.

Eggs build the structure of our baked goods in two main ways: emulsifying and stabilizing.

Let's start by taking a closer look at the science of the emulsification process.

Emulsification is the process of diffusing two liquids that don't mix (also called immiscible liquids) into one cohesive mixture. For example, oil doesn't mix with water. Think about a salad dressing you mix vigorously; it's only a matter of minutes before the tiny droplets of oil bind together and find their way back to the top as they separate themselves from the water.

That's because water's molecules are hydrophilic (they like to be in water), but the oil's molecules are hydrophobic (they dislike water and like to be in fat).

Now, when we mix in the eggs during the baking process, we also add lecithin found in the egg yolk. The lecithin acts as the binding agent, also known as a surfactant, and its structure is made of a hydrophilic head and a hydrophobic tail.

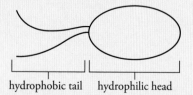

hydrophobic tail   hydrophilic head

A closer look at the structure of a lecithin molecule.

When we add those tiny surfactants, they find a place between the water and the droplets of fat. The hydrophilic head is in the water, while the hydrophobic tail is in the fat. As a result, the oil droplets are mixed into the liquid and don't bind together and separate themselves from the liquid—as they normally would without the presence of eggs.

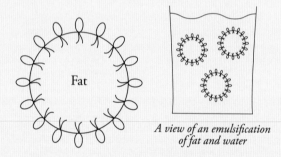

A view of an emulsification of fat and water

But what about egg whites? Even though egg whites don't contain any lecithin, they actually use their protein structure to bind—to emulsify—in the same way.

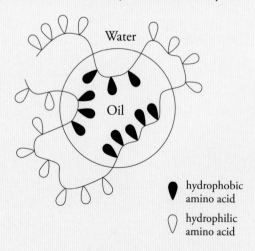

● hydrophobic amino acid

◯ hydrophilic amino acid

An egg white molecule unfolded, repositioning itself so that the hydrophilic amino acids are facing the water while the hydrophobic molecules are positioned in the oil.

This is the melted butter mixed with sugar, but without the eggs. See how the butter and sugar are separated?

When the sugar and butter are mixed along with the eggs, we get a cohesive smooth mixture.

When the batter is fully mixed and ready to be baked, it should be cohesive, with no excess oil.

Egg whites' proteins are long chains that are part hydrophilic and part hydrophobic. In their natural state, those chains are folded, but when we whisk the egg whites, the chains are unfolded (think of a ball of string—you pull at the end and now you have a long unfolded string). Much like surfactants, the proteins reposition themselves, so the hydrophilic parts will find their way in water while the hydrophobic parts will comfortably sit in fat.

It's important to understand that this emulsification process is one of the most important steps in baking. When missing or when not properly incorporated, the fat and liquid don't bind. They separate during the baking process, and as a result, our baked goods will have a weak structure that might not hold themselves together—and a greasy unpleasant texture.

The first step calls for warming the butter and brown sugar together, until the butter has melted and the brown sugar has dissolved. Once the brown sugar dissolves, it absorbs the liquids from the melted butter and its surroundings and is considered to be an invert sugar (syrup), a liquid. It's very clear to see that no matter how hard or for how long we mix the two together, the butter will not fully mix in with the sugar.

To fix this, we simply mix in the eggs with the sugar and butter, and sure enough, we have a smooth cohesive mixture. When we look at the batter before or the blondies after baking, it will be impossible to clearly identify oil, flour or any other ingredients.

If we did not add the eggs, or add the flour mixture before adding the eggs, the water and fat would not mix together properly or at all. We would end up with greasy, lumpy blondies, where we'll be able to identify which parts of the cookies are fat and which are flour—instead of the chewy, tender and flavorful blondies that we want!

The Caramelized Banana Blondies recipe on the next page is a great example of how to use emulsification in your baking to create the ideal smooth and chewy blondie texture.

(continued)

NOTE

Eggs are one of the most common ingredients in emulsification, but the molecules in milk also facilitate emulsification! See The Secret Ingredient for Stabilizing Whipped Cream (page 36) to learn more about emulsifying with milk.

CARAMELIZED BANANA BLONDIES

These chewy and flavorful blondies are a great way to showcase how eggs emulsify and contribute to the texture of our baked goods.

YIELD: One 8 x 8–inch (20 x 20–cm) pan of blondies

¾ cup plus 1 tbsp (184 g) unsalted butter, divided

1¼ cups (250 g) light brown sugar

1 large banana

2 cups (250 g) all-purpose flour

½ tsp cinnamon

½ tsp salt

1 large egg

1 large egg yolk

1 tsp vanilla extract

1½ cups (252 g) butterscotch chips

1 cup (117 g) chopped toasted walnuts or pecans

Preheat the oven to 345°F (173°C) and line one 8 x 8–inch (20 x 20–cm) square pan with parchment paper. Set aside.

In a medium pan over medium heat, melt ¾ cup (170 g) of the butter and the sugar. Then, pour the mixture into a large bowl and allow it to cool as you get the rest of the ingredients ready.

Peel and split the banana lengthwise down the middle. Then, melt the remaining 1 tablespoon (14 g) of butter over medium heat in a sauté pan. Use a paper towel to gently tap the side of the banana to soak up any liquid, then sauté the banana for 1 minute on each side, or until it's lightly browned. Remove from the heat and place on a plate to cool.

In a large bowl, sift together the flour, cinnamon and salt. Mix the egg, egg yolk and vanilla into the butter-sugar mixture until completely blended and smooth; this is where the emulsification technique comes in. Then, mix in the flour mixture. Mix in the chips and walnuts or pecans, then evenly spread the batter into the prepared pan.

Place the banana on top of the batter and gently press it down into the batter. Bake for 30 minutes. Twenty minutes into baking, check the blondies and make sure the banana is not too dark. If it is, cover the pan with aluminum foil. Make sure to remove the foil as soon as you take the pan out of the oven. The blondies are ready when the top is light golden brown and it's puffed all the way to the center.

Remove from the oven and allow for the blondies to cool completely before removing and slicing. The blondies should be stored covered at room temperature for up to 3 days.

HOW EGGS BUILD YOUR BAKED GOODS' STRUCTURE (cont.)

The second way that eggs build structure in our baked goods is by stabilizing them.

We take so much pride when our cakes rise tall and maintain their beautiful exterior, but did you ever think about why our cakes don't fall apart once they're cooled down? That's because eggs are there to stabilize them!

Let's get into the science of stabilizing:

Eggs are made of part egg whites (that are 88 percent water and 10 percent protein) and part egg yolks (that are 50 percent water, 30 percent fat and emulsifiers and 17 percent proteins).

When eggs are in a raw form, they're liquid; we can pour them much like we do water. That's because of the state the protein molecules are in and how they're dispersed.

As we've discussed, eggs' proteins are long chains of thousands of amino acids that are bonded together. Some of the amino acids love to be in water (hydrophilic) and some dislike to be in water (hydrophobic).

When eggs are raw at a temperature that's lower than 140°F (60°C), their molecules have no energy to move, so they're folded in a way that the hydrophobic amino acids are facing each other and away from the water. The hydrophilic amino acids are facing toward the water. As long as the molecules are folded, they will be separated from each other and simply float in the water (see illustration).

Once we add energy by applying heat or by mixing the eggs, the folded protein chains bump each other and eventually unfold, a process that's called denaturing. When the molecules are unfolded, the hydrophobic amino acids are fully exposed to water, so they're making their way toward other hydrophobic amino acids and away from the water. When they find each other, they stick together. In the same way, the hydrophilic amino acids will make their way toward other hydrophilic amino acids and toward the water—and eventually stick together.

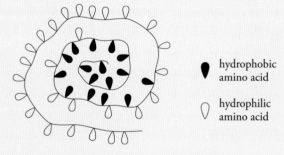

hydrophobic amino acid

hydrophilic amino acid

A protein molecule in its folded state

A denatured (unfolded) protein molecule

The process of the amino acids sticking to each other after the denaturing is called coagulation. It's what creates a stabilized and complex net. Water gets trapped in the gaps between the bond of proteins, thickening the solution and eventually creating a complex net of the egg's protein that stabilizes our baked goods and keeps them from collapsing. We can see this net at work whenever our cakes, cookies and even softer treats like Key Lime Mousse (page 29) hold their shape. We can hold them in our hands or use a spoon to eat them.

The denaturing process can start as soon as we beat the eggs; however, for the eggs to coagulate, heat needs to be provided. Egg whites tend to coagulate faster than egg yolks and at a temperature of 140°F (60°C), while egg yolks begin to coagulate at a temperature of 150 to 160°F (65 to 70°C). When we add ingredients such as milk, sugar and flour, the temperature at which the coagulation process starts will increase. That means we need to apply more energy by increasing the cooking temperature.

If we overheat the egg mixture or over-beat it, the amino acids will bond so tight they will squeeze the water out and break the structure. We see that many times when our custard is dry, curdled and when some unpleasant liquid deposit fills the bottom of the baked good.

The following Key Lime Mousse is a great example of how eggs stabilize and thicken a baked good. The recipe uses eggs in two ways: first, by applying heat and cooking egg yolks and second, by incorporating air into the egg whites. Though these different methods result in different products—one is curd and the second is meringue—on the molecular level, the process is the same.

We first make the lime curd using only egg yolks. We mix them with the sugar to start the denaturing process, then we apply heat to fully coagulate the eggs, which we can easily see when the mixture becomes thick and opaque. The rich, flavorful egg yolks will not only stabilize and thicken the mixture, but they will also add flavor (after all, fat is flavor) and a smooth, dense and creamy texture to any baked good.

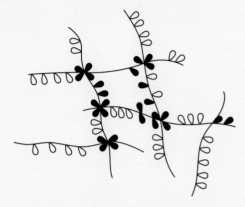

This is what a coagulation of denatured protein molecules looks like. It forms a gelatin net, which traps liquid in between the gaps.

Next, we make the meringue with the egg whites, which is made of lots and lots of tiny air bubbles trapped in between the unfolded proteins. We start the denaturing process by beating the egg whites only on medium-low speed. Next, as the egg whites begin to unfold and trap air, we add the sugar and continue whipping until a stiff meringue forms.

As we fold the light and airy meringue into the dense lime curd, we actually incorporate air bubbles that, as a result, lighten the curd and create an airy mousse.

This mousse is so light and airy it melts in the mouth as it coats it with creamy texture and delicious, sweet and tangy flavors. The whipped cream is added for extra flavor and to balance the strong lime flavor.

It's important to allow the mousse to rest overnight. Once we mix the curd, meringue and cream together, the molecules first reposition themselves in between the air bubbles, creating body, then they will set, holding that body. This is what gives the mousse a firm yet light and airy texture.

KEY LIME MOUSSE

This light and airy key lime mousse is a wonderful example of how eggs help hold our desserts together, through the coagulation and the denaturing process.

YIELD: **Six 4-ounce (113-g) dessert cups**

CURD

½ cup (120 ml) fresh-squeezed key lime juice

2 tbsp (12 g) key lime zest, divided

6 large egg yolks

⅓ cup (66 g) granulated sugar

1 tbsp (14 g) unsalted butter

WHIPPED CREAM

⅔ cup (160 ml) heavy cream

1 tbsp (15 g) granulated sugar

MERINGUE

6 large egg whites

½ tsp cream of tartar

1 cup (200 g) granulated sugar

GARNISH (OPTIONAL)

½ cup (120 ml) lightly whipped cream

¼–⅓ cup (25–34 g) graham crackers crumbs

In a medium saucepan, place the key lime juice with 1 tablespoon (6 g) of the zest and cook it over medium heat. While the juice is cooking, mix together the egg yolks and sugar. Have within reach a large sieve over a clean large bowl (large enough to fold the cream and meringue).

Once the juice comes to a boil, pour 2 tablespoons (30 ml) of the juice at a time into the egg mixture while constantly stirring. Pour the mixture back in the pan and cook on medium-low while constantly stirring until it has thickened, 1½ to 2 minutes.

Run the curd through the sieve, then add the remaining zest and butter. Stir until the butter has melted, then cover with plastic wrap and place in the refrigerator to cool and set for 2 to 3 hours. When the curd has set, whip the cream and sugar until the cream has thickened. Then, fold it into the curd mixture. Place it back in the refrigerator while you make the meringue.

Place the egg whites in the bowl of a stand mixer fitted with the whisk attachment and beat on medium-low speed. Add the cream of tartar and gradually increase the speed to medium-high for about 2 minutes, or until a thick and light foam forms. Sprinkle the sugar in three stages, counting to 10 between each addition to allow the sugar to dissolve. Increase the speed to high and beat until a glossy stiff meringue forms, 5 to 7 minutes.

Fold the meringue into the key lime mixture, then fill a large piping bag with the mixture. Pipe the mixture into dessert cups and place them in the refrigerator to set overnight. Garnish with lightly whipped cream and crushed graham crackers (if desired).

The mousse can be kept in the refrigerator for up to 3 days.

How Starches and Other Ingredients Thicken Baking

Ingredients like starches (flour, cornstarch, potato starch, etc.), gelatin, tapioca and agar agar powder are known in baking as thickeners.

Thickeners are ingredients or methods we use in a solution to increase its viscosity, meaning how fast or slow it moves. Water has a low viscosity, while milkshakes have a high viscosity.

Starches, like flour and cornstarch, are one of the most common ingredients used to thicken a mixture. Add it to your mixture, then apply heat, and it'll thicken.

For example, milk has a low viscosity, since it pours easily and fairly fast. But, if we cook ¼ cup (31 g) of all-purpose flour into 1 cup (240 ml) of milk, much like in the following Old-Fashioned Buttercream recipe (page 32), we'll have a thick product that will pour very slowly.

Here's a look into the science behind this change: When heated with a liquid, the starch granules swell up and absorb the liquid around it. This change in size leaves much less room for the now swollen starch molecules to move around, therefore thickening the liquid. In addition, the starch molecules also release long carbohydrate chains that bond to each other and form a gelation network, which traps liquid in between, thickening the mixture.

Other ingredients commonly used for thickening are gelling agents such as gelatin (sourced from animal protein), agar agar powder (sourced from seaweed) and tapioca (sourced from cassava roots).

Like starches, these gelling agents will begin to thicken a mixture once heat is applied. As the temperature rises, the molecule strands move around rapidly, and as the solution cools, the strands slow. As they do, they curl and tangle around each other, trapping liquid in between the gaps.

The tangled bond of the strands is very delicate and breaks even with the smallest increase of temperature. This quality is what provides a pleasant mouthfeel as the solution melts in our mouths.

Note that both gelatin and agar agar powder should be mixed with water ("bloom") before being added to the solution. This step helps provide an even distribution of the substance into the solution, and without it, it will be clustered.

Reduction refers to the process of reducing the liquid in a mixture; therefore, reducing the space the molecules have to move around.

When we bake, we almost always use some kind of thickener. Our cakes, cookies and cupcakes are full of flour starches that swell during baking time and eggs that coagulate into a gelation network. The fruits in our pies are thickened with tapioca or cornstarch and we reduce the water content when we make caramel. So, the thickening process is very much present in all aspects of baking, and without it, we would most likely have to drink our desserts versus actually eating them.

The ingredients we use to thicken the delicious Old-Fashioned Buttercream (page 32) are what give it its smooth, creamy texture. Without thickening, it wouldn't be possible to create a frosting texture that can be spread and piped.

In this recipe, we cook 1 cup (240 ml) of milk with flour and cocoa powder, allowing the starches to swell and thicken the milk. We'll add the flour mixture into the butter and sugar mixture. This is, in fact, thickening by emulsification. As we incorporate the butter into the flour mixture, tiny droplets are created that thicken it and eventually give us a smooth buttercream.

NOTE

It's very common for the buttercream emulsification to "break," and when that happens, the buttercream looks curdled. There could be a few reasons for that—a change in the temperature, the buttercream is too old. If that happens, make sure to bring the buttercream to room temperature, then beat it in the bowl of a stand mixer fitted with the paddle attachment on medium speed for 4 to 5 minutes, or until it's smooth again.

OLD-FASHIONED BUTTERCREAM

This smooth and stable chocolate buttercream is a great example of how starches thicken mixtures and contribute to our baking process.

YIELD: 3 cups (840 g), enough to frost 12 cupcakes or one 8-inch (20-cm) cake

2½ tbsp (20 g) all-purpose flour

4 tbsp (20 g) cocoa powder

1 tbsp (7 g) dried milk powder

1 cup (240 ml) milk

1¼ cups (284 g) unsalted butter, room temperature

1 cup (200 g) granulated sugar

Mix the flour and cocoa powder. Add the dried milk powder to the milk and stir. Then, mix in 4 tablespoons (60 ml) of the milk mixture into the flour-cocoa mixture. Use a fork to mix the milk into the flour-cocoa mixture, then gradually pour in the remaining milk and mix until smooth and there are no lumps.

Pour the milk mixture into a medium saucepan and cook over medium heat while constantly stirring, until the mixture has thickened, 1 to 2 minutes. Remove the mixture from the heat, pour it into a bowl and cover with plastic wrap until fully cooled.

In the bowl of a stand mixer fitted with the paddle attachment, beat the butter and sugar on medium-high speed for about 5 minutes, or until light and fluffy. Scrape the bottom and sides of the bowl and add the flour-milk mixture. Beat for an additional 5 minutes, or until completely smooth and the sugar has dissolved.

It's best to use the buttercream immediately or store it at room temperature for up to 3 days

*See image on previous page.

Elevate Your Piecrust's Texture with Starch

In this chapter, we learned how driers—such as starches—are ingredients that help build a structure in baked goods. The way they do that is by absorbing the moisture in their surroundings and by minimizing the fluidity of the batter and/or dough.

When we take a closer scientific look, we can better understand how driers like potato starch not only help build a structure, but how they can help improve the texture of our baked goods—like piecrust.

Let's recall how in the section about flour (page 17), we talked about the importance of gluten, how it forms and what texture we can expect from a well-developed dough. We know that the structure of the gluten network is one of the baking foundations and it's the base on which cakes, cupcakes, cookies, pies and most breads rely.

When we bake piecrust, we wish for a tender, sometimes flaky crust that can hold its structure without crumbling. To do that, we have to create the perfect balance of a firm yet delicate gluten network. That way when we roll and fill the dough, it has a structure that can hold its shape and, at the same time, slices easily and melts in our mouths as we bite it.

This is why the type of flour that we use when making piecrust is so important: the lower the protein percentage the better. Pastry flour, which has a low percentage of protein, is highly recommended for baking pies, but it's hard to find, not very economical and, unless you are a savvy pie baker, you might find it hard to work with.

Another great option is bleached all-purpose flour, which also has a lower percentage of protein (many of us don't like to use it due to health concerns). Unbleached all-purpose flour is a great, common and economical option, but I find that it tends to form too strong of a gluten structure and absorbs more liquid than pie dough calls for.

The solution is super easy and quite surprising. Since flour is mostly starch, the way to minimize the gluten development in our all-purpose flour is to increase the starch percentage by adding 3 tablespoons (21 g) of potato starch to our flour. In baking, starch is referred to as a drier, and it's also a substance that weakens gluten.

How?

By absorbing the liquid that otherwise would be absorbed by the protein (gluten), and that causes it to form a strong gluten network that might result in a tough and chewy texture. The molecules in potato starch are much smaller than the flour molecules, so even adding a small amount like 3 tablespoons (21 g) to our recipe helps us elevate the piecrust texture!

My favorite way to use this piecrust recipe is as part of a butternut squash galette with caramelized onion! It's the most rewarding breakfast, brunch, lunch or dinner dish. It features a layer of sweet cinnamon-flavored caramelized onion and is topped with slices of butternut squash and raisins, all wrapped up in that sturdy yet tender and buttery crust.

The great news is that you don't have to limit yourself to the use of the drying effects of starch to just pie (see My Favorite Homemade Donuts on page 80). Adding it to cakes, cupcakes or different recipes that call for all-purpose flour is a great use of your new knowledge of driers in the baking world.

BUTTERNUT SQUASH– CARAMELIZED ONION GALETTE

This tender, unique galette further demonstrates how driers like starch help build structure in baked goods (like piecrust!) by absorbing extra moisture and stabilizing the dough.

YIELD: **One 9-inch (23-cm) galette**

CRUST

1½ cups (188 g) all-purpose flour

3 tbsp (21 g) potato starch

⅛ tsp baking powder

¼ tsp salt

½ cup (114 g) unsalted butter, cold

1 tbsp (15 ml) apple cider vinegar

4–5 tbsp (60–75 ml) ice water, divided

FILLING

4 tbsp (60 ml) olive oil, divided

2 large yellow onions (sliced into ¼-inch [6-mm] strips)

½ tsp ground cinnamon

2 cups (340 g) ½-inch (1.3-cm) slices butternut squash

Salt

Pepper

1 cup (20 g) fresh arugula

¼ cup (36 g) raisins

Sift the flour, starch, baking powder and salt into a bowl and place it in the refrigerator or freezer for a minimum of 30 minutes.

Cut the butter into ½-inch (1.3-cm) cubes and place them back in the refrigerator to cool for 30 minutes.

Place the flour mixture in a food processor and pulse three times (2 seconds for each pulse). Add the butter and pulse again eight times, or until the butter is the size of large peas. Add the vinegar and 4 tablespoons (60 ml) of ice water, then pulse five times until the mixture resembles coarse sand.

The dough is ready when it comes together if pinched between your fingers and the palm of your hand. If it doesn't come together, add another 1 tablespoon (15 ml) of ice water.

Place the dough mixture on a clean work surface and use your hand to bring the dough together. Don't knead the dough. Simply press it together into a disc, then wrap it in a plastic bag and refrigerate for a minimum of 2 hours, preferably overnight, or up to 3 days.

While the dough is chilling, caramelize the onions by warming 3 tablespoons (45 ml) of the oil in a large sauté pan. Add the onion and cook over medium heat while stirring occasionally for 25 to 30 minutes, or until the onions are translucent and golden brown. Mix in the cinnamon and cook on low for an additional 1 minute. Remove from the heat and allow the onions to cool.

Toss the butternut squash with 1 tablespoon (15 ml) of oil, salt and pepper.

Preheat the oven to 400°F (205°C) and line a 13 x 18–inch (33 x 45–cm) large cookie pan with parchment paper.

(continued)

BUTTERNUT SQUASH–CARAMELIZED ONION GALETTE (cont.)

Remove the crust from the refrigerator and lightly dust your work surface with flour. Roll the crust into a 14-inch (35-cm) circle, rotating the dough every two rolls by 90 degrees. Gently fold the dough in half, place onto the prepared pan, then unfold it back into a circle.

Make a layer of the onion, leaving 3 inches (8 cm) of bare edges. Make another layer of squash, then fold the bare edges toward the center.

Bake for 45 minutes, or until the crust is golden brown and the squash is soft. Remove the galette from the oven and allow it to cool for 5 to 10 minutes. Then, sprinkle it with arugula and raisins, slice and serve.

NOTE

You can use cornstarch if you don't have potato starch on hand, but note that cornstarch has a "mealier" flavor to it that might change the flavor of the crust.

The Secret Ingredient for Stabilizing Whipped Cream

Even though it's not scientifically correct to say that the following whipped cream recipe is "caramelized," it helps paint a clearer picture of what the end result tastes like.

It's thick, smooth and full of deep, rich flavors—it can be a dessert of its own. This cream is great to frost cakes and pipe cupcakes with or to even enjoy as is.

What gives this whipped cream a deep, rich and complex flavor is the fact that we browned the dried milk powder (see the Browned Honey Burnt Basque Cheesecake on page 91). The chemical reaction that causes food to brown is different than the one that causes sugar to caramelize (see Create Incredible Caramel Flavor on page 92).

But, more importantly, this whipped cream has a thick, firm texture. This is thanks to the addition of one very important ingredient: dried milk powder!

To better understand the contribution of the dried milk powder, let's take a closer look at the ingredients that make up whipped cream and revisit the fascinating world of emulsification.

Whipped cream, when in its liquid form, is a thick cream that gets its richness from the high concentration of fat globules. Most heavy cream we find at our local markets is 35 to 40 percent fat, with the majority of the remaining ingredients being water. The reason that the fat globules don't float to the top of the water, like most fat would do when we mix it with water, is that the cream contains milk solids. Those milk solids are acting as emulsifiers—binding agents—allowing the fat globules to mix in with the water.

Remember, fat molecules are hydrophobic; they dislike water and only like to be in a fat environment. The same is true for water molecules that are hydrophilic; they like water and only like to be in a water environment. Unlike the fat molecules and the water molecules in cream, the milk solids' molecules don't mind whether they're in a fat or water environment, so they sit at the surface of the fat globules, between the fat and water, preventing the fat globules from binding with each other and separating from the water.

When we add dried milk powder, we add even more milk solids to the cream. They sit at the surface of the fat globules and keep the fat from separating from the water. As a result, the cream can be whipped into a thicker cream with a creamier consistency that will hold together when spread on a cake or piped on a cupcake.

What happens when we whip cream?

When we whip cream, we incorporate tiny air bubbles, and the fat globules (molecules in the shape of droplets) sit around the air bubbles, preventing them from bursting. The more we whip, the more air bubbles we incorporate. Since the amount of water and space doesn't change, the bubbles get smaller and smaller, bringing the fat globules closer together. The increase in air bubbles and decrease of space between the fat globules is what thickens the cream.

It's a known fact that when whipping cream, it's important not to over-whip. If we over-whip, the fat globules might get too close to each other and bind together, separating from the water and breaking the emulsification. In addition, they will squeeze the air out, causing the cream to deflate.

Now, let's take a close look at the "Caramelized" Whipped Cream recipe (page 39) to better understand how we actually get a stabilized browned whipped cream.

The recipe first calls to brown 1½ tablespoons (11 g) of dried milk powder. This is when the Maillard reaction (page 88) takes place and creates a golden color, as well as complex, delicious and rich flavors.

Once we incorporate the dried milk powder with the heavy cream, it's important to allow the cream to fully cool. If the cream isn't completely cool, the fat will not be able to firmly sit and grab the air bubbles. This is also the reason this recipe says to use a cold bowl and a cold whisk.

As mentioned before, as we whip the cream, the fat globules come closer together as we incorporate more and more air into the cream. The fat globules in our cream mixture have extra milk solids coming from the addition of dried milk powder and provide a tighter layer of emulsification. By covering more of the fat globules' surface that will hold onto the air bubbles more tightly, it lowers the risk of the air deflating and of the fat globules binding together.

As a result, our cream has a thicker, more stabilized and fluffier texture due to its ability to incorporate more air.

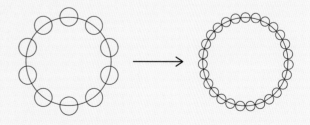

The addition of milk solids increases the number of molecules sitting at the surface between the fat globule and water, increasing the stability of the heavy cream, as you can see here!

"CARAMELIZED" WHIPPED CREAM

This recipe is a great example of how scientific principles like emulsification and the Maillard reaction work to make our sweet treats even better!

YIELD: 1½ cups (90 g) whipped cream

1½ tbsp (11 g) dried milk powder
1 cup (240 ml) heavy cream, divided
2 tbsp (16 g) powdered sugar

NOTES

Do not be tempted to add more than 1½ tablespoons (11 g) of dried milk. Too much will over-saturate the cream and prevent it from creaming.

During the browning of the milk powder, the proteins in the powder coagulate. This is why the powder might clump as we add the cream, but don't worry, it will dissolve slowly as it cools.

Place the dried milk powder in a small saucepan over medium-low heat, then place the cream next to the stove in a measuring cup. While stirring with a wooden spoon, cook the milk powder until it turns light-medium brown in color, a sign that the Maillard reaction is happening. It should take 2 to 3 minutes (make sure to stay close, it might take a while for the powder to brown, but when it does, the change is fast).

Turn the heat off and pour ¼ cup (60 ml) of the cream into the saucepan, stirring until a smooth paste is formed. Then, pour in the remaining ¾ cup (180 ml) of the cream and stir to incorporate. Avoid pouring more than ¼ cup (60 ml) at a time or the powder will clump.

Pour the cream back into the measuring cup and place it in the refrigerator to completely cool.

Pour the cream in the cold bowl of a stand mixer fitted with a cold whisk attachment, add the sugar and whisk, starting on low and gradually increasing the speed to high. Beat until the cream is thick and smooth (this should take 2 to 3 minutes depending on the strength of your mixer).

The cream is ready when the whisk leaves thick strides of smooth cream, much like buttercream. Don't over-whip. Use it immediately or store it in the refrigerator for up to 2 days.

TENDERIZERS:
Ingredients That Create the Ideal Texture in Baking

Tenderizers are ingredients that give our baked goods their soft, moist texture. These ingredients include:

- **Fat**—butter, oil and egg yolks

- **Sugar**—granulated, brown and syrups

- **Acids**—cream of tartar, buttermilk, vinegar

- **Leavening agents**—baking powder, baking soda and yeast

These tenderizers oppose the formation of the strong and tough structure, which stabilizer ingredients (page 16) create. In order to have a successful baked good, you need to balance incorporating stabilizers and tenderizers so your final product has both a firm and stable structure and a moist and tender texture. Not enough tenderizers will result in a tough, dry and unpleasant texture, while too much moisture will cause the product to crumble and fall apart.

Much like the stabilizers, there are quite a few kinds of tenderizers. So, for us to choose the right ingredients, which will tenderize our baked goods without them falling apart, we need to understand the science behind how they work.

In this chapter, we'll take a close look at the molecular structures of these tenderizers, as well as their properties, and learn how to use them in our baking for perfectly tender, moist, soft baked goods.

Fat: The Key Ingredient for Perfect Texture

Fats are substances that don't dissolve in water. Fat is a very common and important ingredient in the baking world—for good reason. Fat's biggest contribution to baking is its ability to tenderize our baked goods by coating the stabilizers (the flour and starches), so when we take a bite, the texture is smooth and tender. More often than not, fat is the key ingredient in many recipes, such as buttercream and brownies.

In baking we use different types of fats, including butter, oil, shortening and more. Each type of fat comes from a different source and has a different molecular structure and behavior. But despite the noticeable differences, all the types of fat unquestionably improve our baking.

Fats are tenderizers.

As mentioned above, they coat the stabilizers and driers. But another way fats help tenderize is by shortening gluten threads, preventing them from forming a long, tight and tough gluten network. In fact, this is the reason behind the names "vegetable shortening" and "shortbread dough"; the high content of fat "shortens" the formation of a long gluten network.

Fats help with the process of leavening.

Fat has the ability to trap air that later, during baking, expands as gas, steam and carbon dioxide, which is then released.

Fats preserve freshness.

As our baked goods cool and are exposed to air, the starches reposition themselves and form new bonds. Those bonds are what begin making our baked goods stale! Luckily, fat has the ability to disrupt the formation of the bonds, helping our baked goods stay fresh for longer.

Fats contribute flavor.

Butter, lard, olive oil, coconut oil and many others are all fats that contribute to the richness and flavor of our baked goods.

Fats thicken and add volume.

Fat is often used as a way to thicken: for example, buttercream. The way to incorporate the fat into the solution and, as a result, thicken it, is with the power of emulsification. Emulsification is a very complex and delicate process (see page 22), and it refers to the process of mixing two elements that will not mix naturally, such as fat and water. Thickening by emulsifying refers to the idea of vigorously adding tiny droplets of fat, whether butter or vegetable shortening, to our object and creating a crowded environment in which the molecule cannot move due to the lack of space. Those tiny droplets not only thicken but also provide a rich, buttery and smooth texture.

You might see a resemblance in the function of fat, a tenderizer, and starch, a stabilizer—they both thicken and add volume. While they both can be used for the same purpose, we need to remember that fat provides a moist tender texture, while starches create a tough texture.

This is a great example of the delicate and complex process of baking and how understanding the science behind it will help us become better bakers.

NOTE

The amount of fat should be 35 to 50 percent of the overall formula. For example, if you're making buttercream, then the butter should weigh the same as the remaining ingredients (such as sugar, eggs and flavoring agents).

Fats provide a moist texture.

Fats help create a pleasant, easy-to-bite texture in our baking.

The most common types of fats used in baking are butter and oil—and you'll learn more about how to use them in the following sections of this chapter—but there is a surprising additional source of fat that can be used to create the ideal texture in our baking.

Let's take a closer look at the Hazelnut Chocolate Cookies (page 44) to better understand. These beautiful little cookies have a thin crispy layer at the top and a soft, chewy texture in the center. The interesting thing is that the recipe doesn't call for any fat or even flour.

So, what gives the cookies that chewy tender texture? The egg yolks. Egg yolks, are 50 percent water, 30 percent fat and emulsifiers and 17 percent proteins.

Fat provides flavor and tenderness to baked goods, so when we add egg yolks to a recipe, we add moisture as well. This is why eggs can technically also be classified as a tenderizer in addition to a stabilizer (page 41)!

You'll notice that the recipe calls to first bake the cookies for 5 minutes at 325°F (160°C), then lower the temperature to 250°F (120°C). Baking the cookies for 5 minutes at 325°F (160°C) will dry up the top of the cookies, and as the cookies expand, those beautiful cracks will form at the top.

We then lower the temperature, because the cookies are small, and if we bake them at a temperature of 325°F (160°C) or higher, we can easily overheat the protein, create a strong coagulation and end up with a dense and tough cookie.

HAZELNUT CHOCOLATE COOKIES

These soft cookies are a great example of how egg yolks act as a tenderizer, adding moisture to our baked goods.

YIELD: 14 cookies

2 cups (250 g) roasted hazelnuts

1⅓ cups (160 g) powdered sugar, divided

¼ cup (55 g) light brown sugar

⅓ cup (29 g) cocoa powder

1 tsp baking powder

¼ tsp ground nutmeg

⅛ tsp ground cardamom

4 large egg yolks

4 tbsp (60 ml) heavy cream

Preheat the oven to 325°F (160°C). Have 14 mini cupcake liners at hand and ready to be filled, placed on a half-sheet cookie pan.

In a food processor, process the hazelnuts and ⅓ cup (40 g) of the powdered sugar until it resembles a coarse meal. Don't overprocess or the nuts will turn to oil.

Place the nuts in a large bowl and add the brown sugar, cocoa powder, baking powder, nutmeg and cardamom and mix to blend. Add the egg yolks and cream and mix, using a spoon or your hands, until a sticky dough forms.

Measure 2 tablespoons (40 g) of the mixture and roll it between your hands to form a ball. Then, roll it in the remaining 1 cup (120 g) of powdered sugar mixture to fully coat it and place it in a mini cupcake liner.

Repeat with the rest of the dough, then place the cookies on a cookie pan and bake for 5 minutes. Reduce the heat to 250°F (120°C) and bake for an additional 15 minutes. The cookies are done when they're puffed and the tops are cracked. Remove from the oven and allow them to cool before serving.

The cookies can be stored at room temperature in a sealed container or cookie jar for up to 5 days.

*See image on page 40.

How to Aerate Butter for Light, Melt-in-Your-Mouth Baking

It's no surprise that when we think about making cakes, we have a clear picture of butter, flour, sugar and eggs. But when we think about the ideal texture of a cake, we imagine a structure that's tender, light and melts in our mouths—and achieving that requires a technique that's a little bit trickier to understand.

Aeration refers to the method by which we add tiny bubbles of air into the butter, eggs or other ingredients when making a cake.

When we take the time and the right steps to perfectly aerate the butter, the result is a much lighter cake with a larger volume, which rises higher and has a more tender texture. A perfectly aerated cake has lots and lots of tiny air bubbles coated with butter that easily burst with flavor in our mouths.

Using granulated sugar, a source of force (a stand mixer, a hand mixer or, if you dare, your arms) and, most importantly, room-temperature butter, let's take a quick closer look at the science behind how butter traps air bubbles. Butter is made up of fat molecules, which cluster in cold temperatures and spread out when you add heat. At room temperature, the fat molecules not only have the ability to separate from each other, but they also have the flexibility to surround the air and trap it.

So how do we do that? How can we trap air—a substance that's invisible, immeasurable and has a very light density—into butter, a dense, fatty substance that doesn't easily mix with other substances?

As we beat the sugar with the butter, the sugar crystals cut into the butter, leaving tiny holes that are quickly filled with air.

The air doesn't escape; it's now trapped within a wall of fat—the butter.

This process takes 5 to 7 minutes if you use a stand mixer and requires quite a force to actually trap the air in the butter, so make sure you use a high speed. Much like when you want to blow out candles, if you blow lightly, the candles will keep on burning since there was not enough force to blow them out.

The following buttery, moist Orange Sesame Cake recipe (page 47) is a great way to practice the aerating technique. We beat the butter and sugar together until the mixture is lighter in color and has doubled its volume. Since we take the time to incorporate as many air bubbles as possible, the air increases the volume of the mixture and lightens the color. These beautiful small bubbles will expand during baking and will give the cake structure and a higher volume, resulting in an impressively tall and tender cake. As the cake cools and sets after baking, the bubbles will hold their shape. That's why when we bite into our cake, it will be tender and light.

ORANGE SESAME CAKE

This amazingly tender treat is how aerating butter creates an ideal cake texture.

YIELD: One 9-inch (23-cm) Bundt cake

CAKE

2 tbsp (28 g) unsalted butter, melted for greasing the pan

9 tbsp (81 g) toasted sesame seeds, divided

2 cups (240 g) cake flour

2 tsp (9 g) baking powder

½ tsp salt

1 cup (240 ml) full-fat sour cream, room temperature

1 tsp vanilla extract

1¼ cups (250 g) granulated sugar

4 tbsp (24 g) orange zest

1⅛ cups (255 g) unsalted butter, room temperature

4 large eggs

SYRUP (OPTIONAL)

1 cup (240 ml) fresh-squeezed orange juice

½ cup (100 g) granulated sugar

Preheat the oven to 350°F (175°C). Using a pastry brush, thoroughly brush a 9-inch (23-cm) Bundt pan with butter, then sprinkle it with 3 tablespoons (27 g) of sesame seeds. Set it aside.

In a medium bowl, sift the flour, baking powder and salt and use a fork to blend the mixture and set it aside. Mix together the sour cream and vanilla and set it aside.

In the bowl of a stand mixer, place the sugar and orange zest. Use a fork to blend the orange zest into the sugar.

Add the butter to the bowl and beat on medium-high speed for 4 to 5 minutes, until the mixture appears light in color and fluffy in texture. Scrape the bottom and sides of the bowl, then add the eggs, one at a time, waiting for each egg to fully incorporate before adding the next. Again, scrape the bottom and sides of the bowl.

Reduce the mixer speed to medium-low, then sprinkle one-third of the flour mixture followed by ½ cup (120 ml) of the sour cream and vanilla. Repeat with the remainder of the flour mixture and sour cream.

Once you add the last part of the sour cream mixture, turn the mixer off and use a rubber spatula to completely incorporate the flour and the remaining 7 tablespoons (63 g) of toasted sesame seeds.

Spoon the batter into the greased pan and bake for 40 to 45 minutes, or until the top is golden and a toothpick inserted into the center of the cake comes out clean.

While the cake is baking, make the syrup, if desired. In a medium saucepan, bring the orange juice and sugar to a boil. Remove from the heat and pour it into a medium measuring cup with a spout. Place it in the refrigerator to cool.

Remove the cake from the oven and immediately pour the syrup over the cake. Allow it to slightly cool for 15 to 20 minutes, then invert the cake on top of a cooling rack or a serving plate.

Store the cake covered at room temperature for up to 3 days.

NOTES

The addition of the syrup is optional, but it's very important that the syrup is very cold when poured over the hot cake. (To learn why, see the Maple Pecan Cake recipe on page 97.)

In the United States, the average size of a large egg is 55 to 60 grams.

When to Use Butter vs. Oil

In "Fat: The Key Ingredient for Perfect Texture" (page 42), we talked about the importance of fat in the baking world and that fat's biggest contribution to baking is its ability to tenderize our baked goods. This is so when we take a bite, the texture is smooth and tender, and more often than not, fat is the key ingredient in many recipes, from buttercream to brownies. This is true whether we're using butter or oil as the fat in our baking.

But still, we don't use butter and oil in the same way. We tend to use butter when we make buttercream, but we're more likely to pick olive oil when baking a rich chocolate cake. The reason why we use one type of fat versus another in different recipes is that each fat has different qualities and appearances.

These differences are very clear to us: We can see them, smell and taste them—even feel them. One of the differences is the source of the fat, where it's coming from. The source of butter is an animal, while olive oil's source is a plant. Each source has a different flavor.

And, of course, the most obvious difference is the state each fat is in—butter is solid while oil is liquid. Let's focus on the science behind these different states of fat.

The melting point for butter is 90°F (32°C). At this temperature, the butter melts and it changes its state from solid to liquid.

The melting point for olive oil is -22°F (-30°C), so at any temperature below, the oil will turn from liquid to solid. This is why we all know oil as a liquid, because most times, oil is stored at a temperature that is higher than -22F (-30C).

There is a huge gap between the melting point of butter and oil. The reason is that butter is a saturated fat, while olive oil is an unsaturated fat.

The molecules of saturated fat all have the same structure, which makes it easy for them to stick to each other at a temperature that's lower than its melting point. For a visual picture, imagine a zipper and how easily it comes together with its match.

On the other hand, the unsaturated fat molecules have the same structure, but they have the addition of one bond, or a double bond along their chain. Think of it like adding another zipper vertically, at the end of our first zipper. The unique and bent shape of the molecules makes it very hard for them to bond and also very easy for them to separate.

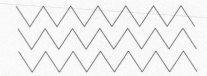

A saturated fat molecule perfectly aligned with other molecules.

In unsaturated fat molecules, the addition of bonds makes it hard for the molecules to align together into a tight bond.

When we apply heat, we increase the energy of the molecules and they start to move, wiggle and separate. If we relate this to our saturated fat molecules, we know that we need to apply much more heat for them to separate and undergo a state transition from solid to liquid than we'd need to apply to an unsaturated fat. That's why there is such a large gap between the melting point of butter and oil—and this is why they react so differently in recipes.

So, when we try to figure out which fat we want to use for our recipe, instead of thinking butter versus oil, we should think saturated fat versus unsaturated fat. The decision of which fat to use should be based on the properties of the fat itself and what those properties do for a recipe.

Saturated fat is great for recipes that call for aerating like in pound cakes, thickening like in buttercream and to create flakiness like in puff pastries. Unsaturated fat is great when we're pressed for time and can't wait for the butter to soften, or when we want to add extra tenderness to our baked goods (see the Olive Oil Chocolate Pancakes recipe on page 53).

But sometimes we don't need to choose. We can have our saturated and unsaturated fats together, like in the Chocolate-Cherry Pop Tarts (page 49).

I decided to go with both butter and olive oil in this recipe because I wanted to enjoy the best of both worlds. If I only use butter, then I will end up with dough that resembles more of a cookie texture—and I wanted it to be a bit softer and more tender. If I use only oil, then the dough will be too soft and not elastic enough to roll and cut. So, I decided to use both butter and olive oil. Together, they will provide their unique flavors while aerating and fully coating the flour, giving us smooth dough that's elastic and, when baked, is tender, soft and crumbly.

CHOCOLATE-CHERRY POP TARTS

This recipe is a great example of when and why to use different kinds of fats.

YIELD: 6–8 pop tarts

POP TARTS

2¾ cups (330 g) all-purpose flour

⅓ cup (29 g) cocoa powder

1 tsp baking powder

1 tsp salt

¼ cup (55 g) light brown sugar

¼ cup (50 g) granulated sugar

7 tbsp (98 g) unsalted butter, cold (cut into ½-inch [1.3-cm] pieces)

5 tbsp (75 ml) milk

1 large egg, beaten

3 tbsp (45 ml) olive oil

FILLING

4 cups (560 g) sweet frozen cherries, thawed and water discarded

½ cup (100 g) granulated sugar

1 tbsp (15 ml) fresh-squeezed lemon juice

1 tsp almond extract

1 tbsp (8 g) cornstarch

1 tbsp (15 ml) water

GLAZE

2 cups (240 g) powdered sugar

2 tbsp (30 ml) water

1 tsp almond extract (optional)

(continued)

CHOCOLATE–CHERRY POP TARTS (cont.)

To make the pop tarts, in the bowl of a stand mixer, sift the flour, cocoa powder, baking powder and salt. Add the sugars, and using the paddle attachment, mix it on low speed to fully incorporate the ingredients, about 30 seconds.

Add the butter and increase the mixer speed to medium high. Continue mixing until the mixture resembles wet sand, then drizzle in the milk and egg, followed by the olive oil. Then mix on low for an additional 45 seconds.

Divide the dough into four equal parts, wrap each part with plastic wrap and place them in the refrigerator for a minimum of 2 hours, preferably overnight. While the dough is cooling, make the filling.

To make the filling, in a medium pan, place the cherries, sugar, and lemon juice and cook over high heat until the sugar dissolves. Stir occasionally. Reduce the heat to medium-low, add the almond extract and keep cooking until the liquid reduces by two-thirds, 25 to 35 minutes. Make sure to stir occasionally.

In a small bowl, stir together the cornstarch and water, then add them to the cherry mixture and cook, while stirring, until the mixture has thickened. Remove from the heat and place it in a container to cool.

To assemble, preheat the oven to 350°F (175°C) and line a large 13 x 18–inch (33 x 45–cm) cookie pan with parchment paper. Place it close to your working area.

Remove one part of dough from the refrigerator, dust your work surface with flour, then roll the dough into a 6 x 9–inch (15 x 22–cm) rectangle. If the dough breaks, knead it for about 20 seconds and try again. Using a sharp knife or a cookie cutter, cut the dough into three 3 x 4–inch (8 x 10–cm) rectangles.

Using a small offset spatula, gently place the dough on the prepared pan, brush the edges of each rectangle with some water (you can use your finger or a small paintbrush), then add 1 tablespoon (16 g) of the filling at the center of two rectangles.

Layer another piece of cut dough on top of the cherry-filled dough and use a fork to press the edges together. Once done, use a toothpick to score the pop tarts at the center four or five times. Then, place them in the refrigerator while the oven is warming.

Bake the pop tarts for 14 to 15 minutes. They're done when they look dry and the edges are brown. Remove them from the oven and allow them to completely cool before glazing.

To make the glaze, mix the ingredients together. Use a spoon to glaze the pop tarts. At this point, the pop tarts are ready to be eaten and will stay fresh for up to 2 days.

How to Choose the Best Oil for What You're Baking

I would say that the best way of eating the following delicious Olive Oil Chocolate Pancakes (page 53) is as a big pile loaded with syrup, fresh berries and nuts. These pancakes are so moist and tender, all thanks to the addition of olive oil.

Oil, whether it's vegetable oil or olive oil, is one of the greatest ways we can very easily achieve a tender and moist crumb in baked goods. If you've ever baked with oil, then you must know that cakes and other items baked with oil are significantly more moist and much more tender.

But why is that?

Well, oil has two very important qualities that can really help us understand what is going on. First, at room temperature, oil is liquid; you can pour it very easily into the batter. And second, oil is 100 percent fat; it doesn't contain any water, milk solids or emulsifiers.

When it comes to baking, the softer and more liquid the fat source is, the more easily it makes its way into the batter, coating flours, starches and protein particles. As we learned in the Stabilizer chapter (page 16), flour and eggs are considered to be stabilizers in baked goods—they provide structure and stability. So, naturally, if we coat those particles with fat, we'll tenderize them and, as a result, have a tender crumb.

Since oil is 100 percent fat—therefore, does not contain water—as we mix it in there is no concern of increasing the formation of gluten bonds.

Choosing oil when baking is a great option when a recipe doesn't use fat as a source of aeration (see the Orange Sesame Cake recipe on page 47). It's a great substitution for melted butter, and sometimes it's added in addition to butter to ensure a moist and pleasant texture. If you choose to replace melted butter with oil, make sure to use 85 percent of the amount of butter the recipe calls for.

Just like with butter, flavor plays a great part when choosing which type of oil to use. Olive oil is known for its "earthy" notes, and it tends to pair wonderfully with chocolate, as it enhances its flavors, like in the pancakes.

Of course, it's a personal preference, and you can experiment and have fun using different types of oil such as vegetable oil, avocado oil, walnut oil, grapeseed oil and more.

OLIVE OIL CHOCOLATE PANCAKES

This recipe is a great example of how to choose the best oil for what you're baking.

YIELD: 8 pancakes (amount may vary depending on size)

¾ cup plus 1 tbsp (100 g) all-purpose flour

¼ cup (22 g) cocoa powder

⅓ cup (66 g) granulated sugar

2 tsp (9 g) baking powder

⅔ cup (160 ml) milk, room temperature

1 large egg, room temperature

1 tsp vanilla extract

2 tbsp (30 ml) olive oil

¼ cup (57 g) unsalted butter, divided, to butter the pan

½ cup (120 ml) chocolate syrup

1 cup (120 g) assorted berries

In a medium bowl, sift together the flour, cocoa powder, sugar and baking powder, then mix to blend.

In a separate bowl, mix the milk, egg, vanilla and oil, then pour it over the flour mixture. Use a fork or a wooden spoon to mix just until incorporated (a few lumps are okay).

Place a flat pan over medium heat and melt ½ teaspoon of butter. Use a clean paper towel to clean any excess butter; this step is important because excess butter will make it hard to flip the pancakes.

Pour ¼ to ⅓ cup (60 to 80 ml) of batter in the pan and reduce the heat to medium-low (this amount is for a medium-sized pancake). Cook for 2 to 3 minutes, or until the sides of the pancakes appear dry and you notice some bubbles on top. Flip the pancakes and cook for an additional 30 seconds.

Serve immediately. The pancakes are best drizzled with chocolate syrup and fresh berries.

*See image on next page.

NOTE

You can make the pancakes in any size you wish. The cooking time will vary, so pay attention to the appearance of the pancakes.

HOW TO CHOOSE THE BEST OIL FOR WHAT YOU'RE BAKING (cont.)

Your desired texture will also determine what kind of oil you should choose. Let's get into the science behind why:

In the previous recipes, we learned that the main differences between each type of fat are the source, flavor and whether it's saturated or unsaturated. The molecules of saturated fat bind together easily and stay solid at a much higher temperature than unsaturated fat. Since unsaturated fat molecules don't bind together easily, they become a solid only at very low temperatures—when they have almost no heat (energy) stopping them from bonding.

But not all unsaturated and saturated fats have the same melting point temperature. Below, you can see the different types of oil commonly used in baking and their melting points.

Butter	89–95°F	32–35°C
Cocoa butter	93°F	34°C
Coconut oil	77°F	25°C
Lard	105°F	41°C
Olive oil	21°F	-6°C
Peanut oil	37°F	3°C
Sunflower oil	1.5°F	-17°C
Canola oil	14°F	-10°C
Grape seed oil	50°F	10°C

Palm oil	95°F	35°C
Flaxseed oil	12°F	-11°C
Almond oil	32°F	0°C

So if you want your baked goods to truly melt in your mouth, then you should choose an oil with a melting temperature lower than the temperature of your mouth, which is our natural body temperature of 97°F (36°C). That's what I've done in the Triple Coconut Cake recipe (page 56).

This cake actually does melt in your mouth, since we use coconut butter, which has a melting point of 75 to 78°F (24 to 26°C). This means it will melt pretty fast at room temperature and, in fact, it will melt even faster in our mouths. This means that when we bite into the cake, the oil will literally melt, giving us an incredibly tender cake texture that you'll fall in love with.

The coconut oil is incorporated into the recipe along with the butter, in its solid form, and it also helps the butter with the aeration process. It also provides an amazing coconut flavor.

If you'd like to try another recipe that takes advantage of this technique, check out the Classic Peanut Butter Cookies (page 110).

TRIPLE COCONUT CAKE

This recipe is a great example of how to use different oils' melting points to create melt-in-your-mouth cake texture.

YIELD: **Two 3 x 8–inch (8 x 20–cm) cakes**

3⅓ cups (400 g) all-purpose flour

2 tsp (9 g) baking powder

½ tsp baking soda

⅓ cup plus 1 tbsp (100 ml) full-fat sour cream, room temperature

1¼ cups (300 ml) full-fat coconut milk

1 tbsp (16 g) vanilla paste or extract

½ cup (114 g) unsalted butter, room temperature

⅓ cup (85 g) solid coconut oil, room temperature

1 cup (200 g) granulated sugar

4 large eggs, room temperature

1 cup plus 2 tbsp (103 g) unsweetened shredded coconut, divided

Preheat the oven to 350°F (175°C) and line two 3 x 8–inch (8 x 20–cm) loaf pans with parchment paper. Set aside.

In a medium bowl, sift the flour, baking powder and baking soda. Stir to combine. Set aside. In a large measuring cup, place the sour cream, milk and vanilla and mix to combine. Set aside.

In the bowl of a stand mixer fitted with the paddle attachment, place the butter, coconut oil and sugar and beat on medium speed until you have a fluffy and light mixture, 4 to 5 minutes. With the mixer still on medium speed, add the eggs one at a time, waiting for each egg to fully incorporate before adding the next one. Scrape the bottom and the sides of the bowl.

With the mixer on medium-low speed, add the flour mixture in three stages, alternating with the liquid mixture in two stages. Start and finish with the flour mixture. Once you've added the last part of the flour, turn off the mixer and use a rubber spatula to fold in 1 cup (93 g) of shredded coconut and any flour residue.

Divide the batter between the two prepared pans, sprinkle with extra coconut and bake on the middle rack for 45 to 55 minutes, or until the tops of the cakes are puffed and golden brown and a toothpick inserted into the center of the cake comes out clean.

The cake should be stored covered at room temperature for up to 3 days or frozen for up to 2 months.

NOTES

Use a high-quality canned, full-fat coconut milk.

Avoid using coconut milk that is a milk substitution.

Everything You Didn't Know About Sugar

In baking, we think of granulated sugar, also known as sucrose, mostly as a way to add sweetness to our baked goods. But there is so much more to know about it than that! Once we take a closer look at sugar's scientific makeup and properties, we can learn how to best use it and the other ways in which it can improve our baking.

Sugar is a firm crystal.

Sugar has a molecular structure that's made of one fructose molecule and one glucose molecule. The strong bond between the two molecules is what gives sugar its crystal shape and firm texture. When we press it, it stays solid and doesn't change its structure.

Sugar dissolves in water.

Sugar dissolves in water to the ratio of two to one: 2 cups (400 g) of sugar will dissolve in 1 cup (240 ml) of water. When sugar is dissolved in water, it becomes an inverted sugar—which we know better as syrup.

However, when we heat or boil the water, the sugar's solubility, its ability to be dissolved, increases so much that we can melt up to 4 cups (800 g) of sugar in just 1 cup (240 ml) of water.

When you wish to make simple syrup, you can use the same amount of water and sugar or increase the sugar up to four times. The more sugar you add, the higher the viscosity (thickness) of the syrup will be—it will be thicker and will pour slower.

Sugar melts and caramelizes.

Sugar melts at 365°F (185°C) and begins to caramelize at 320°F (160°C), so when sugar melts, it's a caramelized sugar—a key component of caramel! This is why many caramel recipes call to mix the sugar with some water and allow the sugar to dissolve in the water and gradually increase the temperature for a slow, more even caramelization process.

Sugar has no flavor, but sweetens other flavors.

Sugar provides sweetness but no flavor unless it's caramelized. Make sure to add flavor from other sources such as chocolate, lemon, vanilla, etc.

Sugar is a hygroscopic substance.

A hygroscopic substance is a substance that's able to absorb water from its surroundings. Sugar has an affinity to water, and when sugar absorbs water, a strong bond is formed between the sugar and water molecules that slows down the evaporation of moisture, providing a moist and tender product.

A very simple yet unique and delicate recipe that relies on and uses many of the sugar qualities we talked about above is the Simple Syrup Rose Water Jell-O (page 60).

To make this recipe, we start with boiling some water with sugar, creating simple syrup. We use 1 cup (240 ml) of water and 1 cup (200 g) of granulated sugar, but you can reduce or increase the amount of sugar as you please depending on your personal preferences.

Since sugar doesn't provide any flavor, a very small amount of rose water is added. Without the sweetness from the sugar, the rose water would taste very soapy and unpleasant.

In this recipe, we dissolve the sugar in water to make an inverted sugar—liquid syrup. We thicken and firm the syrup with gelatin, so we can enjoy eating it as a dessert.

This recipe is easy and simple, but it melts in the mouth and leaves a very subtle and sweet flavor coming from the rose water.

The rosebuds floating in the cups are optional. If you choose to use them, know that they will float to the top if mixed right away, before the syrup has a chance to slightly thicken. So, allow the mixture to thicken for 2 to 3 hours before pouring it into the serving cups and mixing it with the dried rosebuds.

Once you mix in the gelatin, avoid over-stirring the syrup. Over-stirring will scatter molecules more and the syrup will turn from transparent to opaque.

(continued)

SIMPLE SYRUP ROSE WATER JELL-O

This recipe is a great example of how to use the properties of sugar to create unique treats!

YIELD: 1½ cups (63 g) Jell-O

1½ tsp (8 g) unflavored gelatin

1 cup plus 1 tbsp (255 ml) water

1 cup (200 g) granulated sugar

½ tsp rose water

5–6 dried rosebuds

In a small bowl, mix the gelatin and 1 tablespoon (15 ml) of water and allow the gelatin to bloom while you make the simple syrup.

Place the remaining 1 cup (240 ml) of water and sugar in a medium saucepan and bring to a boil, stirring occasionally. Once boiling, reduce the heat to low and cook for an additional 2 minutes. Meanwhile, warm the bloomed gelatin in the microwave for 3 seconds.

Remove the simple syrup from the heat and pour it into a large heat-resistant bowl. Gently stir in the rose water, then the gelatin. Allow the simple syrup to cool at room temperature for 2 to 3 hours, until it starts to thicken but can still be poured into the cups.

Crumble a rosebud (or two, depending on the size of the dish) into your choice of dessert cup, then slowly pour in the simple syrup mixture. The rosebuds tend to rise to the top of the syrup, which is why it's important for it to thicken before pouring over the rosebuds.

Place the dessert cups in the refrigerator to chill and set, 1 to 2 hours. They can be stored in the refrigerator for up to 2 days.

*See image on previous page.

EVERYTHING YOU DIDN'T KNOW ABOUT SUGAR (cont.)

We can use what we've learned about sugar's properties for better baking results—this time using them to add moisture to a blondie recipe!

When we bake brownies, the high percentage of chocolate and cocoa powder is what gives the brownies their dense and rich texture. But there's no chocolate or cocoa butter when we bake blondies, and so with the following Browned Butter–Coffee Blondies (page 63), we rely on the sugar to provide us with a texture that's close to a brownie.

As we know, sugar is a hygroscopic substance; it likes water and absorbs it from its surroundings. In this recipe, we use ⅔ cup (145 g) of light brown sugar and ⅓ cup (66 g) of granulated sugar (sucrose). Brown sugar is sucrose that's coated with inverted sugar—syrup, and in most cases, molasses syrup. An inverted sugar is even more hygroscopic than sucrose, so when we add brown sugar to a recipe, we add extra flavor and moisture.

We take an extra step by allowing the light brown sugar and granulated sugar to sit in the melted butter mixture. During that time, the granulated sugar absorbs the water coming from the mixture and, as a result, it turns into an inverted sugar. When we take a closer look at the molecular level when the sugar absorbs the moisture, the sucrose bond breaks into separated fructose and glucose molecules, which results in a softer and not brittle texture.

In addition, the fructose molecules tend to caramelize at a lower temperature of 350°F (175°C), providing us with more flavor.

You'll notice that the recipe calls for 1 teaspoon of cream of tartar. The reason is that as the blondies are cooling down, the cream of tartar will prevent the fructose and glucose molecules from bonding back together and crystallizing, which, as a result, would give the blondies a crisp texture rather than the moist texture we're going for. See page 69, The Softest Double Chocolate Chip Cookies, for another example of how to use cream of tartar to create softer baked goods.

By using our new scientific knowledge and sugar's properties, we're able to bake these chewy, tender blondies. You can also apply your understanding of sugar to create recipes of your own! The unique texture of the blondies—along with the flavors coming from the browned butter and caramelized sugar and the coffee flavors—makes these blondies a delicious, one-of-a-kind experience.

BROWNED BUTTER–COFFEE BLONDIES

This recipe is a great example of how sugar can add moisture to baked goods.

YIELD: 16 blondies

1 cup (227 g) unsalted butter, divided

1 cup (220 g) light brown sugar

½ cup (100 g) granulated sugar

1 tsp instant coffee

2 tsp (10 ml) vanilla extract

2 large eggs

2 cups (250 g) all-purpose flour

1 tsp cream of tartar

1 tsp salt

1 cup (168 g) chocolate chips

1 cup (109 g) chopped pecans

Preheat the oven to 350°F (175°C) and line one 8 x 8–inch (20 x 20–cm) square pan with parchment paper. Set aside.

In a medium saucepan, melt ½ cup (114 g) of butter and allow it to cook until there is a thin layer of foam on top and the butter has a light brown color to it and a nutty aroma.

Remove the butter from the heat and pour it into a large mixing bowl. Cut the remaining ½ cup (114 g) of butter into 1-inch (2.5-cm) pieces and add them to the browned butter. Gently stir until the butter has fully melted. Add the sugars and mix. In a small bowl, dissolve the instant coffee in the vanilla. Add the eggs and stir until fully incorporated.

Let the mixture sit for 10 minutes, but gently mix every 2 minutes. Meanwhile, in a separate large bowl, sift the flour, cream of tartar and salt.

Mix the dry ingredients into the butter-sugar mixture in three additions to allow the flour to be fully absorbed. Mix in the chocolate chips and pecans, then spread the batter into the prepared pan, using an offset spatula to even it out.

Bake for 30 to 35 minutes, or until a thin, dry layer has formed on top. Remove the pan from the oven and let cool for 15 to 20 minutes before removing the blondies from the pan and slicing.

The blondies should be stored at room temperature in a sealed container for up to 4 days or in the refrigerator for up to 1 week.

What Is Acid and How Does It Better Our Baking?

Acid is one of the most common ingredients used in baking and it's used very often, more than we actually realize in the baking world. The most common acidic ingredients used in baking are sour cream, buttermilk, honey, vinegar, yogurt, wine, coffee, cream of tartar and more.

Let's learn more about the science behind what makes an ingredient an acid! On a daily basis, we measure the acidity of an ingredient on a pH scale. Ingredients below 7 are considered to be acidic, over 7 are not acidic (they're basic) and 7 means they're neutral.

Apple cider vinegar's pH level is between 2 to 3, meaning it's acidic. Water's pH level is 7, meaning it's neutral, and egg white's pH level is between 7.5 to 9.5, meaning it's basic.

An ingredient's acidity is measured by how easily its molecules release their hydrogen ions in water. Hydrogen ions are the particles that hold the positive charges of certain molecules. Think of it like a fist holding coins: the fist is the molecules and the coins are the hydrogen ions. When the molecules are wetted, the fist opens and the coins are released. Different molecules release their hydrogen ions at different rates. High-acidity molecules that make up the acid ingredients we use in baking will release their hydrogen ions much faster than nonacidic molecules.

Why do we need to know this? Because we can take advantage of acid's amazing properties when we're baking, such as:

Acid weakens gluten formation.

Every gluten molecule has both negative and positive charges, just like the batteries we use in our TV remotes. We connect the positive charge (+) to the negative charge (-) for the remote to work. When we do the opposite and connect the positive charge with the positive charge or the negative charge with the negative charge, the charges repel each other and the remote doesn't work. Acidic food has positive charges, so when we add acid to our batter, we lower the pH level and release positive charges that bond with the gluten's negative charges and neutralize them.

Now the gluten only has negative charges that repel each other and as a result, the gluten molecules stay away from each other, giving us a tender and crumbly texture. (This is exactly why I like to add apple cider vinegar to my piecrust).

Acid helps stabilize meringue and prevent it from breaking.

Many meringue recipes say to add a small amount of cream of tartar, an acidic powder, to the egg whites to stabilize the foam, but the fact is that it not only stabilizes the foam, it also prevents the foam from breaking.

To stabilize, the cream of tartar releases its positive charge and that neutralizes the negative charges of the proteins in the egg white, because now there are no positive charges to attract the negative charges. As a result, the proteins change their shape from a folded chain to an unfolded chain that coagulates with other chains and traps the air bubbles, creating a foam or a meringue.

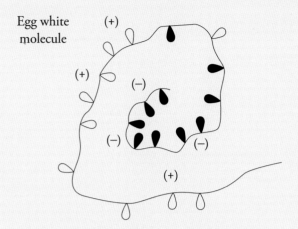

Egg white molecule

(+)

(+)

(−)

(−)

(−)

(+)

In addition to hydrophilic and hydrophobic amino acids, egg white molecules also have negative (-) and positive (+) charges that repel and attract each other, allowing the molecule to keep its folded yet loose structure.

◖ hydrophobic amino acid

◗ hydrophilic amino acid

(+) positive charge   (−) negative charge

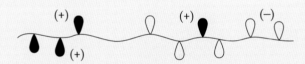

(+)

(+)

(+)

(−)

The positive charges coming from the cream of tartar neutralize the negative charges of the egg white, leaving only positive charges that repel each other, and as a result, the molecule unfolds itself.

Along the protein molecules are sulfur atoms that contain hydrogen ions (think of Christmas lights; the curds are the molecule chains and the lights are the atoms). As the proteins unfold and bond together, the sulfur atoms release the hydrogen ions into the liquid around them. Now, they have the space to bond with other sulfur atoms on other protein chains, strengthening the bond of the protein, and squeeze the air and water out and, as a result, break the foam.

When we increase the pH level by adding cream of tartar, the hydrogen ions in the cream of tartar take the place of the ones the sulfur atoms released, preventing them from binding to other sulfur atoms and breaking the meringue.

Acid balances flavor.

When we taste an acidic food, the hydrogen ions send a sour signal to the brain. Therefore, the addition of acid helps to balance the overwhelming sweetness of sugar. Many candy-makers—and even sweet drinks manufacturers—add acidic supplements to balance the sweetness of their products. I guess that explains why Coca-Cola® has a pH level of 2.5 . . .

Acid helps fruits and vegetables maintain their firmness.

When we cook fruits and vegetables, the walls that surround the fruit's molecules and give fruits their firmness dissolve and, as a result, the fruit starts to tenderize. Those walls are not as soluble in acid as they are in basic ingredients. So, adding acid when baking or cooking fruits will help maintain their shape and firmness.

In the next recipe, we'll also talk about how acid activates baking soda to help level our baked goods, while also providing flavor and moisture.

We can see and taste the amazing contributions of acid in the delicious and incredibly soft and tender Blueberry Snack Cake (page 66). The acidic Greek yogurt activates a chemical reaction along with baking soda, helping to leaven it, and as well as giving it extra moisture and flavor.

The blueberries keep their shape and firmness as they're baked in an acidic batter. And despite the fact that there is as much sugar as flour, the cake isn't too sweet because the acidity of the Greek yogurt balances the sweetness of the sugar.

(continued)

BLUEBERRY SNACK CAKE

This recipe is a great example of how acid's properties better our baking.

YIELD: One 9-inch (23-cm) cake

1¾ cups (219 g) all-purpose flour

2 tsp (5 g) potato starch

½ tsp baking soda

1 tsp baking powder

1 cup (240 ml) plain full-fat Greek yogurt (or full-fat sour cream)

1 tbsp (15 ml) vanilla paste or extract

7 tbsp (98 g) unsalted butter, room temperature

1 cup (200 g) granulated sugar

¼ cup (60 ml) vegetable oil

2 large eggs, room temperature

1⅓ cups (197 g) fresh blueberries, divided

⅓ cup (36 g) sliced almonds

Preheat the oven to 320°F (160°C). Grease and line the bottom of one 9-inch (23-cm) pan with parchment paper and set aside.

In a medium bowl, sift together the flour, potato starch, baking soda and baking powder and set aside. In a large measuring cup, mix together the yogurt and vanilla paste or extract. Set aside.

In the bowl of a stand mixer, beat together the butter and sugar on medium-high speed until light and fluffy, about 3 minutes. Scrape the bottom and sides of the bowl, then drizzle in the oil. Add the eggs, one at a time, allowing for each egg to fully incorporate before adding the next. Once the eggs fully incorporate, add the flour mixture in three additions, alternating with the yogurt mixture, but starting and ending with the flour.

Stop the mixer and fold in ⅓ cup (49 g) of the blueberries with the batter, then evenly spread the batter into the prepared pan. Sprinkle the remaining blueberries on top, then sprinkle the almonds.

Bake for 45 to 48 minutes, or until the top of the cake is lightly golden and a toothpick inserted into the center of the cake comes out clean.

Remove the cake from the oven and allow it to cool for 10 to 15 minutes before serving. The cake is best eaten the same day and can be stored at room temperature for up to 2 days.

WHAT IS ACID AND HOW DOES IT BETTER OUR BAKING? (cont.)

A very special and often overlooked acid in baking is cream of tartar. Cream of tartar, also known as potassium bitartrate, is an acidic byproduct of wine-making and is mainly known as a key ingredient in baking powder (see page 64). But in a baker's kitchen, cream of tartar takes on a much more complex role that's often overlooked—softening baked goods.

In our kitchen, we mostly use sucrose, which is a scientific name for table sugar or granulated sugar. It's made of one molecule each of fructose and glucose. Sucrose dissolves during the mixing and baking process, then crystallizes into coarse sugar crystals as it cools—this is what gives candy and many other baked goods a crispy and brittle texture.

But when a solution of sucrose is heated in the presence of cream of tartar, the acid breaks the bond between the fructose and glucose and creates an inverted sugar, a term that refers to any liquefied sugar (syrup) such as corn syrup, maple syrup, molasses, honey and glucose syrup. Unlike granulated sugar, inverted sugar doesn't crystallize, which is why cookies baked with inverted sugar will set into soft, tender cookies.

So, adding a fairly large amount of cream of tartar to your recipe, like we do with The Softest Double Chocolate Chip Cookies (page 69), will turn the granulated and light brown sugar into an inverted sugar (syrup) and we'll get the softest-ever cookies. These cookies are not just the softest chocolate cookies, they're also chubby, loaded with chocolate chips and they crumble and dissolve into the most tender and delicious blast of chocolate as we bite into them.

What gives these cookies their addictively tender texture is the addition of cream of tartar.

THE SOFTEST DOUBLE CHOCOLATE CHIP COOKIES

These soft and tender cookies are a great example of how cream of tartar's properties work to better our baking!

YIELD: 15 large or 24 medium cookies

1⅔ cups (208 g) bleached all-purpose flour

1 tsp baking powder

⅓ cup (29 g) unsweetened cocoa powder

2 tsp (8 g) cream of tartar

1½ cups (252 g) chocolate chips

1 large egg

1 large egg yolk

2 tbsp (30 ml) milk

1 tsp vanilla extract

1 cup (227 g) unsalted butter, room temperature

¾ cup (165 g) light brown sugar

¼ cup (50 g) granulated sugar

Preheat the oven to 350°F (175°C) and line two 13 x 18–inch (33 x 45–cm) cookie sheets with parchment paper.

In a medium bowl, sift together the flour, baking powder, cocoa powder, cream of tartar and chocolate chips and use a fork to fully blend. Set aside. In a small bowl, mix together the egg, egg yolk, milk and vanilla. Set aside.

In the bowl of a stand mixer on medium-high speed, beat together the butter and sugars until light and fluffy, 4 to 5 minutes. Scrape the bottom and sides of the bowl, so it doesn't fly out of the bowl.

With the mixer speed on medium-high speed, drizzle in the egg mixture. Once fully incorporated, add the flour mixture and beat just until the flour has been fully incorporated. You can increase the mixer speed to high, but make sure the flour is mostly incorporated first so it doesn't fly out of the bowl.

Use a large cookie spoon (holds 3 tablespoons [45 g]) to scoop the dough, leaving 3 inches (8 cm) of space between each cookie to allow them to spread. Bake for 10 to 12 minutes if using a dark-colored cookie sheet or for 12 to 14 minutes if using a light-colored cookie sheet.

The cookies are done when they're puffed and no longer appear wet in the center.

NOTE

You can use a medium cookie spoon as well (holds 1½ tablespoons [22 g]), but please note that the smaller the spoon is, the less the cookies will spread. Make sure to adjust the baking time to 8 to 10 minutes or 10 to 12 minutes.

It's important to know that due to the relatively large amount of acid in this recipe, the protein and flour will set fast, so these cookies don't spread much and keep a "chubby" figure.

Boost Your Baking with Leaveners

Leavened baked goods are baked goods that a source of aeration (page 45) has been added to. They're light, tender and have a much more airy texture than unleavened baked goods. A pound cake (see the Almond-Chocolate Pound Cake recipe on page 118) is a leavened cake. It rises high and is very crumbly, but blondies (see the Browned Butter–Coffee Blondies recipe on page 63) are unleavened and are packed very densely, with a chewy bite.

There are three ways to leaven our baked goods: by using chemical leaveners like baking powder and baking soda, by using yeasts and by incorporating liquid into the batter and dough.

Leavening occurs when gas expands the air bubbles that have been incorporated into the batter or dough during the mixing process.

Where are the air and gas coming from? In baking, we actually incorporate the air during every step of the mixing process, whether intentionally like when aerating the butter with sugar (see page 45 for an explanation of the aeration process) or unintentionally like when sifting the flour and kneading the dough.

So, by the end of the mixing process when our object is ready to be baked, it's full of tiny air bubbles, which sometimes are enough to leaven baked goods by themselves.

But often, baked goods need a little extra help to leaven—this is where leaveners like baking powder, baking soda and yeast come in handy.

These leaveners produce carbon dioxide gas when heat is applied. This gas is really light, so it wants to make its way up to a place with a similar light environment—like those air bubbles that we incorporated into our batter. As the air makes its way into the air bubbles, it expands them even further. The water in the batter also turns into steam during the baking process (see page 12 for more information), which helps the gas expand the air bubbles. This expanding of the air bubbles is what leavens our baked goods.

Now that we understand the basics, let's dive a little deeper!

Chemical leaveners—baking soda and baking powder—are highly concentrated powders that come in handy when a long fermentation time for yeast activation isn't an option and an additional source of gas is needed for our batter.

Baking soda (sodium bicarbonate) is the base for all chemical leaveners. It's a powder that, along with an acidic substance and moisture, produces carbon dioxide gas. There are two ways we can apply baking soda in our baking. The first one is by activating the baking soda with a source of acid, such as buttermilk, and the second one is by using baking powder.

Baking soda by itself isn't acidic at all—it's alkaline. So, when we add it to baked goods, it might help spread and brown our baked goods, but it doesn't leaven them.

However, when we mix baking soda with an acid, the chemical reaction of one acid molecule along with one baking soda molecule produces one molecule of carbon dioxide gas (CO_2), two molecules of water (H_2O) and one molecule of salt residue (CH_3COONa).

$$\text{Baking Soda + Acid} =$$
$$2(CO_2) + 2(H_2O) + 1(CH_3COONa)$$

This CO_2 gas, as we know, leavens our baked goods. But the reaction between baking soda and an acid also produces water molecules, which contribute to the moisture of the cake and some salt molecules that contribute to the flavor of the cake. As a result, you'll get a much moister and more flavorful cake by utilizing this scientific reaction!

Baking soda is very common and highly economical—and we can easily find a source of acid in our kitchens. Here are some equally common acidic ingredients you can use to activate baking soda: sour cream (like I use in my Nutty Bread recipe on page 72), buttermilk, yogurt, cottage cheese, fruit juices, honey, brown sugar, unsweetened chocolate, cream of tartar, vinegar, molasses, wine and alcohol and carbonated soft drinks.

A general rule of thumb is that ½ teaspoon of baking soda will be activated by 1 cup (240 ml) of fermented milk, 1 teaspoon of lemon or vinegar and 1¼ teaspoons (6 g) of cream of tartar (page 69).

The following Nutty Bread gets its delicious flavors and tender, crunchy texture from the browned butter, macadamia nuts, walnuts and white chocolate chips. But what truly makes this bread so moist, light and tender that it melts in your mouth as you bite into it is the combination of baking soda and an acid (sour cream).

In this recipe, one cup (240 ml) of sour cream, activates the ½ teaspoon of baking soda. That reaction, along with the baking powder, will leaven the quick bread, allow it to rise and give it a light texture. The chemical reaction will also add an addition of moisture, giving the quick bread a tender texture and adding a depth of flavor.

This quick bread, at first sight, seems dense and heavy, but once you bite into it, it simply melts in your mouth and fills it with complex, deep flavors of browned butter, nuts and white chocolate chips.

(continued)

NUTTY BREAD

This recipe is a great example of the reaction that happens when we combine baking soda and an acid, and how we use it to create incredible texture in our baked goods.

YIELD: One 5 x 9–inch (13 x 23–cm) loaf

½ cup (114 g) unsalted butter (cut into 1-inch [2.5-cm] pieces)

1⅔ cups (200 g) all-purpose flour

¾ tsp baking powder

½ tsp baking soda

1 cup (220 g) light brown sugar

1 cup (240 ml) sour cream, room temperature

2 large eggs, room temperature

¾ cup (126 g) white chocolate chips

½ cup (59 g) chopped toasted walnuts

½ cup (60 g) chopped macadamia nuts

Preheat the oven to 325°F (160°C) and line one 5 x 9–inch (13 x 23–cm) loaf pan with parchment paper and set aside.

Place the butter in a medium pan over medium heat. Cook until a thick layer of foam fills the surface and the butter changes its color to golden brown with some dark speckles. This should take 4 to 5 minutes. Pour the butter in a medium bowl and allow it to cool while you prepare the rest of the ingredients.

In a large bowl, sift the flour, baking powder and baking soda and stir to blend, then mix in the brown sugar. In a medium bowl, mix the sour cream and eggs, then drizzle in the cooled browned butter.

Pour the butter mixture over the flour mixture and, using a large wooden spoon, mix in the ingredients just until combined. This is when the baking soda starts to activate with the sour cream, so make sure your oven is warm and ready to achieve the full effect. Halfway into mixing, add the white chocolate chips, walnuts and macadamia nuts. Don't over-mix (a few lumps are okay).

Spread the batter in the prepared pan and bake for 45 to 50 minutes. The bread is ready when the top is puffed and bounces back when touched and a toothpick inserted into the center of the bread comes out clean.

Remove the bread from the oven and allow it to cool in the pan for 10 to 15 minutes before removing and slicing. The bread can be stored covered at room temperature for up to 3 days.

BOOST YOUR BAKING WITH LEAVENERS (cont.)

Baking powder is a combination of baking soda and another source of a chemical acidic product and it's a great way to leaven baked goods.

It's important to know that not all baking powders are created equal, and the type of leavening acid that's present makes a big difference in the quality and taste of our baked goods. For example, baking powder that's mixed with cream of tartar doesn't leave any flavor residue, but the reaction time is immediate during mixing, and by the time we place the batter in the oven, the gas may have already evaporated.

However, baking powder that's mixed with a leavening acid that contains aluminum, such as sodium aluminum pyrophosphate, will have a slow release, but it'll also release a bitter, metallic aftertaste.

So when you purchase your next baking powder, make sure that the container is labeled as aluminum-free and double-acting, meaning that the part of the acid present is activated and reacts with the baking soda in the presence of heat.

The following Monday Night Football Cookies recipe (page 77) is a great example of how baking powder helps with leavening and gives us tender and crumbly cookies.

I created these one late Sunday night when I noticed that a full day of watching football left us with bowls and bags full of leftover crumbs of potato chips, peanuts and some uneaten chocolate bars. I figured my savory-loving better half would enjoy some sweet and salty treats for his upcoming Monday night football routine.

I really wanted the cookies to be light and chubby, but the addition of 3 cups (225 g) of crushed potato chips and peanuts made for a dense cookie dough that required more to leaven it than just aerating the butter with the sugar. This is where baking powder came in handy.

Unlike cake and cupcake batter, cookie dough is much denser and has a much lower water percentage. (That's why it's so easy to eat raw! Unlike cake and cupcake batter, which is much more liquid.) Furthermore, cookie dough's short baking time and high baking temperature don't allow for the water in the batter to fully turn into steam, as it does in cake batter (see page 12 for more information). That lack of steam means our air bubbles will have trouble expanding, and our cookies won't leaven. But not only that: The air bubbles have pressure pushing down on them, from the dense dough, and therefore have a high risk of bursting without something pushing back to maintain the balance.

To better explain this, think of a balloon you just blew up. If you take the balloon and place heavy blankets and pillows on top of it, they will put pressure on the balloon and it might pop. You need a balance of equally strong pressure inside the balloon to counteract the outside pressure from the blankets and pillows.

In baking, the balloon is the air bubbles and the blankets and pillows are the different molecules in the cookie dough. When a batter has a light structure, like meringue foam (page 128), there isn't as much pressure on the air bubbles, so the balance is maintained. But in this cookie dough, the structure is much denser and much heavier, which puts more pressure on the air bubbles.

Pre-baked air bubbles, surrounded with different molecules adding pressure risking bursting.

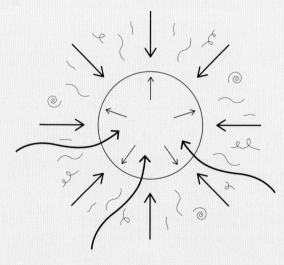

During baking, carbon dioxide gas coming from the baking powder, expands the air bubbles and as a result balances the pressure from the outside, eliminating the risk of the bubble bursting.

So now we have two issues: not enough steam to expand the air bubbles and a strong pressure that might burst the bubbles, leaving us with a dense, unpleasant cookie texture.

Baking powder is the magic solution! Adding 1 teaspoon of baking powder will produce enough carbon dioxide gas to expand the air bubbles even without steam, which will maintain the balance of pressure on the air bubbles, allowing our cookies to leaven correctly.

One important tip to remember: When we mix the baking powder in with the dry ingredients, the baking powder dissolves in the batter during the mixing process. Then, the reaction that produces carbon dioxide gas occurs in the oven once the batter's temperature is increased. This is why we can chill cookie dough without the risk of losing the baking powder's ability to activate.

Now we can understand why only aerating heavy cookies like the Monday Night Football Cookies isn't enough. Mix-ins like potato chips, peanuts and chocolate bar pieces will increase the density of the dough and might deflate the air bubbles we incorporated during mixing. Luckily, we can use the science behind baking powder to expand the bubbles and maintain their balance, leaving us with tender, fluffy, sweet and salty cookies for our Monday night football game.

Rule of Thumb

Use 1 teaspoon of baking powder for every cup of flour.
Add an addition of ½ teaspoon of baking powder for every cup of add-ons like sugar or nuts.
½ teaspoon of baking powder will activate 1 cup (240 ml) of acidic substance (sour cream, buttermilk, yogurt).
You can replace 2 teaspoons (10 g) of baking powder with ½ teaspoon of baking powder and 1 cup (240 ml) of acidic substance.

MONDAY NIGHT FOOTBALL COOKIES

This recipe is a great example of how baking powder helps leaven our baked goods!

YIELD: 20 cookies

2 cups (240 g) cake flour

1 tsp baking powder

½ tsp salt

2 large eggs

1 tsp vanilla extract

1 cup (227 g) unsalted butter, room temperature

¾ cup (150 g) granulated sugar

½ cup (110 g) light brown sugar

2 cups (150 g) finely crushed potato chips, unflavored, divided

2 tbsp (18 g) chopped toasted peanuts

1 cup (169 g) milk chocolate chips

20 pieces of mini twisted pretzels for garnish

Preheat the oven to 350°F (175°C) and line two 13 x 18–inch (33 x 45–cm) cookie pans with parchment paper.

In a large bowl, sift the flour, baking powder and salt. Mix to blend and set aside.

Mix together the eggs and vanilla and set aside.

In the bowl of a stand mixer fitted with the paddle attachment, beat the butter and sugars on medium-high speed until light and fluffy, 4 to 5 minutes. Scrape the bottom and sides of the bowl, then slowly drizzle in the egg mixture while still beating on medium-high. Scrape the bottom and sides of the bowl again, then add the flour mixture on medium-low speed.

Mix in 1 cup (75 g) of potato chips, the peanuts and the chocolate chips and chill the dough for 30 to 45 minutes. Have the remaining potato chips ready in a deep bowl and the mini pretzels next to it.

Remove the dough from the refrigerator, and using a medium cookie spoon (holds 1½ tablespoons [22 g]), scoop the cookie dough, then roll it in the potato chips. Place the cookies on the prepared pans (the dough should be cool and easy to hold with your fingers), gently press a pretzel in the center of the cookie and repeat with the rest of the dough. Make sure to leave 2½ to 3 inches (6 to 8 cm) of space between the cookies to allow them to spread.

Bake for 12 to 14 minutes, until the cookies are puffed and the edges are lightly golden. Remove the cookies from the oven and let them cool for about 10 minutes in the pans before moving to a cooling rack.

The cookies can be stored in a sealed container for up to 5 days.

BOOST YOUR BAKING WITH LEAVENERS (cont.)

Another way to leaven baked goods is with yeast, also known by its scientific name *Saccharomyces cerevisiae*. It's a single-cell microorganism that breaks sugar into two molecules of carbon dioxide (CO2), two (C2H5OH) molecules of alcohol and flavor molecules (the amount varies according to the formulas).

$$\text{Yeast} + \text{Sugar} =$$
$$2(CO2) + 2(C2H5OH) + \text{Flavor Molecules}$$

When activated, each yeast cell feeds on the sugar in the recipe, and as a result, they release gas that leavens the dough and also splits into two separate cells every 2 hours or so. This process is called fermentation and requires a moist environment with the ideal temperature of 78 to 82°F (25 to 28°C).

At a temperature below 32°F (0°C), the yeasts are inactive, so it's the ideal storage temperature. Just remember that the yeasts won't work at this temperature. At a temperature higher than 140°F (60°C), the yeasts die and the fermentation process stops.

There are three types of yeasts:

Compressed yeasts are sold in blocks and are about 30 percent yeast and need to be dissolved in warm water and sugar before being added to the recipe.

Active dry yeast and **instant yeast** both have the same gray, grainy appearance, and both have been dried and vacuumed-packed. However, the process of drying the active dry yeast is much more aggressive than the process of drying instant yeast and results in a large amount of dead yeast that release glutathione, a substance that interferes with the formation of gluten. Active dry yeast should also be dissolved in water and sugar, while instant yeast can be added to the formula with the flour and other dry ingredients.

Let's take a closer look at the following homemade donuts recipe (page 80) and further understand yeast's role in it.

As you can see in this recipe, much like many other bread recipes, there are two steps to create smooth and elastic dough we can later roll and shape into donuts.

Step one is the mixing process; this is when we introduce the flour to the water and yeast. At this point, the starches start to absorb the water and the yeast starts to feed on the sugar. It's best to use a stand mixer fitted with the paddle attachment or a wooden spoon for an optimum distribution of the water to hydrate the dough.

Once the flour has been fully hydrated, we can switch to the dough hook or use our hands as we begin the second step: the kneading process. This is when the gluten development starts as the dough is stretched, pressed and folded many times and in many directions. As we do this, we can very easily notice how the dough transforms from a shaggy mass into a stiff, stretchable dough.

At this point, it's very important that we pay close attention to the development of the dough. As we already discussed on page 17, as we mix the ingredients, the gluten chains get closer and bond long and strong chains. If we mix too much, the chains will get stronger and closer and will result in a chewy and tough dough. But if we don't mix enough, the chains might be too weak to trap the gas that the yeast produced and we'll end up with undeveloped dough with a "yeasty" smell coming from the alcohol molecules that were left behind.

The way to know whether our dough is just right is by pinching a small piece and slowly stretching it with our fingers. If it stretches easily to about 1½ inches (4 cm) before it tears, you know it's ready.

This is when the dough is ready for the fermentation process. The activity coming from the gas production is what helps further strengthen and develop elastic dough.

In this recipe, our mixing process involves creating a sponge. A sponge refers to the process of activating the yeast by initially mixing it with some milk and a small amount of sugar. As the yeast starts to activate and releases gas into the solution, it creates a spongelike mixture. The reason being is that when we make rich dough, we use a large amount of sugar (over 10 percent, see page 80) and it slows the fermentation process by more than one hour. Making the sponge, as well as using a fairly large amount of yeast, helps the yeast adapt quicker to this high sugar environment.

The fermentation process in which the yeast feeds on the sugar and releases gas causes our dough to rise and, eventually, our donuts to be full and chubby. But note that as we increase the temperature during baking—or frying, in this case—and the yeast dies, it sings one last song and releases gas for the last time, helping the dough puff up even more. In addition, the alcohol molecules turn into steam with the increase of heat, which also contributes to the expanding of the dough.

In this recipe, because we made a sponge and used a large amount of yeast, the fermentation process is fast and requires a total of 3 to 4 hours of rest time, the donuts are chubby, tender and fluffy—and they taste amazing with or without glaze.

MY FAVORITE HOMEMADE DONUTS

This recipe is a great example of how yeast works to leaven our baked goods.

YIELD: 12 donuts

DONUTS

1 cup (240 ml) warm milk (90–100°F [32–38°C])

¾ cup (150 g) granulated sugar, divided

1½ tbsp (20 g) active dry yeast

3¼ cups (400 g) all-purpose flour

1 tbsp (7 g) potato starch

½ tsp salt

2 large egg yolks

4 tbsp (56 g) unsalted butter, melted and cooled

Oil spray to grease the dough

1¼ quarts (1.2 L) vegetable oil for frying

GLAZE

2 cups (240 g) powdered sugar

4 tbsp (60 ml) milk

In the bowl of a stand mixer, place the milk, 2 tablespoons (30 g) of the granulated sugar and the yeast. Mix and let sit for 15 to 20 minutes, until the yeast has been activated and the mixture has a thick bubbly layer on top.

Sift together the flour, potato starch, remaining sugar and salt, then add it to the yeast mixture. With the mixer fitted with the paddle attachment on low speed, add the egg yolks and butter and mix until a shaggy mass has formed. Replace the paddle attachment with the dough hook and mix until a smooth dough comes together, 4 to 5 minutes. Lightly spray the dough with oil spray, then cover it with plastic wrap and allow it to rest and rise for 75 to 90 minutes, or until it's doubled in size.

Place the dough on a clean work surface and have a large baking pan ready with ten 4 x 4–inch (10 x 10–cm) squares of parchment paper. Using a rolling pin, roll the dough into a 9 x 9–inch (23 x 23–cm) square about 1 inches (4 cm) thick. Use a 3-inch (8-cm) donut cutter to cut the donuts and place each donut on a piece of parchment paper on the pan. Lightly spray each donut with oil spray, cover the pan with plastic wrap and allow the donuts to rest and rise for 1 to 1½ hours. Allow the leftover dough to relax for about 20 to 30 minutes before re-rolling it to make more donuts. In a deep, wide pan, warm the oil to 325°F (160°C), gently pick up a donut with the parchment paper and place it in the oil, with the parchment paper facing up. Fry each donut for about 1 minute, then remove the paper and fry for an additional 30 seconds. Turn the donuts using a fork and fry for another 90 seconds. Remove the first donut and cut it to check if it's done. This test will be your time mark. If the donut is done, keep frying each donut for 90 seconds total on each side; if not, add 30 seconds of frying time for each side. Mix the powdered sugar with the milk in a large and wide bowl, then dip each donut in the glaze. The donuts should be served shortly after they're done and will stay fresh for 1 day.

TEMPERATURE:
The Force That Transforms Ingredients into Baked Goods

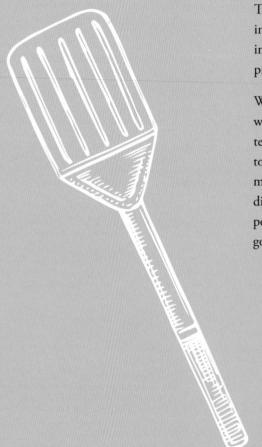

The process of baking means integrating different ingredients, like the ones we've been learning about in the previous two chapters, to create a cohesive new product. How do we do this? By using temperature.

We tend to think that the temperature is only important when it's time to place the baked goods in the oven. But temperature is much more than that! Using temperature to bake does mean adding heat at times, but it also means extracting heat—cooling or freezing our ingredients to get a delicious treat. That's why ice cream and popsicles—and even frosting—are technically baked goods (page 111)!

Temperature is a quantified way (a number) of showing how much energy we add or remove from our ingredients. A change of energy relates to a change to the molecules' behavior. Meaning, when we increase temperature, then we apply energy, and, as a result, the molecules start to move around and interact with each other. When we reduce the temperature, then we reduce the energy, and the molecules stop moving and stop interacting with each other.

Every material has its own molecular interaction behavior that changes with the increase or decrease of its temperature. That's why a temperature change causes an ingredient to undergo a state transition from solid to liquid, from liquid to gas and vice versa.

Let's take, for example, water. Water boils at 212°F (100°C), freezes at 32°F (0°C) and is liquid at room temperature, 75°F (24°C). In each phase, the molecule's interaction behavior is different. At room temperature, the water molecules are in liquid form. They're organized but still have some space to move around. As we increase the temperature, the molecules undergo a state transition from liquid to gas by disorganizing and moving around and away from each other as they absorb heat/energy. We know water in its gas form as steam.

When we lower the temperature, the water molecules are undergoing a state transition from liquid to solid, moving closer together in an organized way, like an ice cube.

We can use this understanding of temperature's effect on water molecules to understand the effect of temperature on other ingredients, such as butter. When baking a cake, many recipes call for you to cream the butter with the sugar when the butter is at a temperature that's not too cold or too warm, anywhere between 70 to 75°F (20 to 24°C); when it is soft to the touch and our finger can leave a dent. This is because if the butter is too cold, its molecules will be too closely packed together, so it will be too solid to mix in with the sugar. If the butter is too warm, the molecules are separated from each other, and in a liquid state, it will dissolve the sugar, making it impossible to incorporate air into the butter.

Understanding the science behind temperature and the effect it has on the molecules' behavior will help us to figure out how to integrate our ingredients in the best way, to give us the best versions of whatever baked goods we'd like to make!

We'll learn and practice this using our knowledge of temperature explained in this chapter. In the following recipes, we'll take temperature into consideration during all phases of the baking process: from the very beginning, starting with getting our ingredients ready to mix, rise and bake; during the baking process; and, finally, during the cooling process.

How to Keep Your Cheesecake from Cracking

Creating the smoothest and creamiest cheesecake all comes down to temperature. Since heat is energy, when we bake our cheesecake in the oven, that warm environment gives energy to the protein molecules, causing them to unfold (denature) and bond (coagulate) with each other into a cross net that holds liquid between them. This is the process that sets the cheesecake and gives it its texture. Therefore, if we want to get the best, moistest and creamiest cheesecake, we need to apply just the right amount of heat to make that happen.

Not enough heat will not allow the molecules to unfold and coagulate, and as a result, we'll end up will an unset cheesecake. Too much heat and the delicate net might break, causing the molecules to bond with each other too tightly and squeeze the water out. This results in a cheesecake with a curdled appearance, dry custard accompanied by an unwelcome liquid deposit and maybe even a cracked top, because now that the liquid is no longer trapped in between the molecules, it will evaporate out the top, causing the cake to crack.

There are a few ways to control the amount of heat that goes into our cake, but first, let's understand the science around how heat travels from the oven into our cake.

When we place our cake in the oven, the heat will only reach the top of the cake and the bottom and the sides of the pan. What happens then is that the energy from those exposed parts "wakes" up the molecules and they start to unfold, wiggle, move around and randomly bump into each other in all directions—up, down, left and right. Think of it like a crowd at a concert that starts to dance when the music begins to play. That bumping creates a random "energy spreading" and it will start from the edges, where the heat from the oven hits the cake directly, and will work itself toward the center of the cake. As long as the cake is in the oven, the process will continue.

This process is called heat diffusion—also known as the "random-walk" theory. The longer the cake is in the oven, the more energy the molecules will absorb, and as a result, move around and randomly bump into each other, and the cake will continue to bake. In fact, even when we turn the oven off, the cake will continue to bake from the outside in, since it takes time for the cake to actually cool.

By watching the edges of the cake, we actually use this theory to control the temperature during baking time and achieve a silky-smooth cheesecake. Once 1½ inches (4 cm) from the edges of the cake are set, it's time turn the oven off and allow the cake to continue baking through the process of heat diffusion.

Another very important step to creating a perfect cheesecake is the cooling process: You should always allow the cake to cool and set in a turned-off oven with the door closed. Removing the cake from the oven before it has a chance to completely cool and set might cause the cake to crack since the molecules are now in a much colder environment and will not have the energy to move. They'll stop, causing any liquid that has yet to set to steam out and crack the cake. Make sure to allow the Funfetti® Cheesecake (page 85), or any other cheesecake you try, to cool in the oven for at least four hours, or until it's completely set and cool.

There are other ways to control the amount of heat the cake gets during baking time as well, and you'll use all of them in the following cheesecake recipe. One is baking the cake at a low temperature of 325°F (160°C), because the less heat the oven provides, the less heat the cake will absorb. The second is using a water bath. Since water evaporates once it reaches 212°F (100°C), then we know that the temperature in contact with the bottom and sides of the cake will not be higher than 212°F (100°C).

All of the above methods—heat diffusion, cooling, baking at a low temperature and using a water bath—are essential and should all be used together for the best results and to create a silky-smooth cheesecake.

The Funfetti® Cheesecake has a smooth top, with no cracks, and a creamy interior. The reason the cake is so creamy with a pleasant texture is because we made sure the cake is baked at a controlled temperature using a low oven temperature and a water bath. Plus, we made sure to take advantage of the science behind heat diffusion by turning the oven off once the edges of the cake have set, despite the fact that the center has yet to. And it's all worth it because by not allowing the cake to overheat, we prevent it from curdling and cracking. The result? A silky-smooth, delicate-tasting cheesecake with a level, even and crack-free top.

FUNFETTI® CHEESECAKE

This recipe is a great example of how to use heat diffusion to keep your cheesecake from cracking.

YIELD: **One 9-inch (23-cm) cheesecake**

CRUST

1½ cups (150 g) graham cracker crumbs

4 tbsp (56 g) light brown sugar

4 tbsp (55 g) unsalted butter, melted

FILLING

4 large eggs

1 tbsp (16 g) vanilla paste

1 cup (200 g) granulated sugar

3 tbsp (24 g) cornstarch

3 cups (696 g) full-fat cream cheese, room temperature

4 tbsp (56 g) unsalted butter, room temperature

1 cup (240 ml) heavy cream, room temperature

½ cup (100 g) sprinkles, color of your choice

TOPPINGS

½ cup (120 ml) heavy cream

1 tbsp (15 g) granulated sugar

3 tbsp (35 g) sprinkles

(continued)

FUNFETTI® CHEESECAKE (cont.)

To make the crust, preheat the oven to 350°F (175°C) and line one 8 x 8–inch (20 x 20–cm) springform pan with parchment paper.

In a food processor, process the cracker crumbs and brown sugar, then add the melted butter. The mixture should resemble wet sand. Pour the mixture into the prepared pan and use the back of a spoon to evenly spread and press it into the pan.

Bake for 8 minutes, then remove the pan from the oven and allow it to cool while you prepare the filling.

To make the filling, reduce the oven heat to 325°F (160°C). In a medium bowl, place the eggs and vanilla paste and mix.

In a separate medium bowl, measure the granulated sugar and cornstarch and mix to blend the cornstarch with the sugar. This step is very important as it ensures the cornstarch will be evenly distributed into the batter.

In the bowl of a stand mixer fitted with the paddle attachment, place the cream cheese and butter and beat on medium speed until smooth, about 1 minute. Then, add the sugar-cornstarch mixture and beat for an additional 3 minutes until smooth. Scrape the bottom and sides of the bowl, then drizzle in the egg mixture in three additions. Allow each addition to fully incorporate before adding the next. Pour in the cream, allow it to blend, then fold in the sprinkles.

Bring 8 cups (1.9 L) of water to a boil for the water bath while you prepare the pan.

Cut two large pieces of aluminum foil about 15 inches (38 cm) in length and place them on the counter crossing each other. Place the pan with the crust in the center, then cover the pan with the foil. This will ensure that no water gets into the pan during baking.

Cut a large piece of aluminum foil about 4 inches (10 cm) longer than the large pan you are using and set aside.

Pour the batter into the pan, then bang it against the counter a few times to make sure there's no air in it. Place the pan in a slightly larger pan. You can use one 2½ x 10–inch (6 x 25–cm) round pan or even a 2½ x 9 x 13–inch (6 x 23 x 33–cm) pan.

Open the oven door and pull out the middle rack. Place the pans on the rack and carefully pour the boiling water into the large pan, making sure it does not get into the pan with the batter. The water should reach to about half the height of the pan with the batter. Cover the pans with the remaining piece of foil and use a knife to pierce four to five holes in it.

Bake for 48 to 52 minutes. The cake is ready when the edges of the cake (about 1½ inches [4 cm] from the sides of the pan) are set but the center still jiggles. Turn the oven off and allow the cake to fully cool in the oven for 4 to 5 hours. Remove the cake from the oven and place it in the refrigerator for an additional 2 hours before slicing and serving.

When you're ready to serve your cheesecake, place it on a serving plate.

To create the whipped cream, beat the heavy cream and sugar until thick. Put the whipped cream into a piping bag, fitted with the rose tip. Then use it to decorate the edges of the cake. Top with the sprinkles!

The cake can be stored in the refrigerator for up to 5 days.

Take Your Cheesecake's Flavor to the Next Level

Just when you think cheesecake cannot taste any better, along comes the Browned Honey Burnt Basque Cheesecake (page 91). It's a cheesy custard swirled with browned honey and baked into a cake with a unique caramel-like flavor all infused into a smooth, melt-in-your-mouth creamy texture.

It's sort of like having two recipes in one because the browned honey is loaded with sweet, complex flavor. You can use it in many other ways too: drizzle it over ice cream, add it to cake batters, use it as filling or just eat it by the spoonful. It's that good!

What gives both the cheesecake and the browned honey such a unique flavor is a chemical process known as the Maillard reaction.

The Maillard reaction is named after Louis Camille Maillard, a French physician who discovered this chemical reaction back in the early 1900s. It's essentially what causes our batters and doughs to brown and creates a beautiful brown crust on our baked goods.

The Maillard reaction occurs when, with the presence of heat, a protein molecule (amino acid) binds with a sugar molecule and creates an unstable structure. That structure then undergoes further changes and, as a result, produces a complex, rich flavor and a brown appearance.

In baking, the protein molecules mostly come from eggs or butter and the sugar molecules come from carbohydrates such as flour or sugar. These ingredients are what cause the Maillard reaction, browning our baked goods and adding a deep flavor.

As you've probably seen in your own baking experiences, only the top, the edges and the bottom of baked goods are brown—never the inside. That's because of the way the water molecules in our baked goods react to heat.

The Maillard reaction happens at a temperature of 248 to 266°F (120 to 130°C). Water boils and undergoes a state transition into steam at 212°F (100°C), meaning as long as water is present, the temperature will not increase to 212°F (100°C) and the Maillard reaction will not occur. This is why only the outer sides of our baked goods are browned. Because heat is applied to our baked goods from the outside in, the exposed parts and the edges that are in touch with the pan are the parts that receive heat directly from the oven and diffuse the energy (see the Funfetti® Cheesecake recipe on page 85) to the center.

Since heat is applied to those areas constantly, the water evaporates during the baking process, allowing the temperature to reach 248 to 266°F (120 to 130°C) and the Maillard reaction to happen. Note that we intentionally prevent the Maillard reaction from reaching the center of our baked goods since water/liquid is a great source for moisture and a tender texture.

Know that the Maillard reaction is very different from caramelization. Caramelization is the browning reaction of sugar—there is no protein involved—and for sugar to be caramelized, the temperature needs to be at a minimum of 325°F (160°C).

We use the principle of the Maillard reaction for both the browned honey and the Browned Honey Burnt Basque Cheesecake.

Let's take a closer look at the process of browned honey. Honey has 1 percent of amino acids (protein), 70 to 80 percent of glucose and fructose (sugar) and about 20 percent of water. The presence of both protein and sugar makes honey a great candidate for browning.

For that to happen, we need to bring the honey to a temperature of 248 to 266°F (120 to 130°C), but that will only happen after the water boils. So, the first step is to bring the honey to a boil and allow the water to evaporate (you know that the water is evaporating once the temperature reaches 212°F [100°C] and over). And once the temperature reaches 248°F (120°C), the browning reaction begins and the flavors start to develop.

I like to allow the honey to reach 266°F (130°C). In addition to more flavors developing, it will be warm enough for the protein in the heavy cream to undergo the Maillard reaction, adding even more flavor.

Now, let's move on to the cheesecake. In the previous recipe, we baked a delicious silky-smooth crack-free Funfetti® Cheesecake (page 85). We did that by controlling the amount of energy the cake absorbed during the baking process. As a result, the cake is tall, light and smooth with no cracks.

But while the relatively low temperature provided an extraordinary texture and intense cheesy flavors, the cake didn't have a chance to undergo the Maillard reaction, which is what gives the Browned Honey Burnt Basque Cheesecake its famous burnt appearance and rich, complex flavors.

In this recipe, we're striving to achieve the opposite effect of the smooth Funfetti® Cheesecake, to create a cracked, burnt-top appearance with a dense texture. To achieve this burnt appearance and the unique flavors, we need to allow the temperature at the surface, the bottom and the sides of the cake to increase 120°F (49°C), which is why we bake this cake at a high temperature of 425°F (218°C).

The high temperature also encourages a fast production and evaporation of steam escaping the cake—causing it to crack. As the steam evaporates, the cake rises by about 2 inches (5 cm), then sinks back down into a dense and creamy texture.

Even though we rely on the high temperature to bake this unique cake, we're still using the same principles of heat diffusion we used to bake the Funfetti® Cheesecake, so we still need to make sure not to overbake it. If we overbake it, the proteins will bond too tightly and, as a result, squeeze the liquid out of the cake—resulting in a dry, curdled cake.

In this recipe, the cake is taken out of the oven once we notice that the cake is tall and puffed and the edges of the cake have set but the center still jiggles when we wiggle the pan, allowing the cake to continue baking using the heat diffusion process.

The cake is so rich and flavorful and should be eaten as is—no add-ons or toppings. Well, maybe an extra drizzle of browned honey wouldn't hurt!

BROWNED HONEY BURNT BASQUE CHEESECAKE

This recipe is a great example of the Maillard reaction and how to use it to create rich complex flavors in your baking.

YIELD: One 8-inch (20-cm) cheesecake

BROWNED HONEY

1 cup (240 ml) honey

½ cup (120 ml) heavy cream

CHEESECAKE

1½ cups (300 g) granulated sugar

1 tbsp (8 g) all-purpose flour

½ tsp salt

3 large egg yolks, room temperature

3 large eggs, room temperature

1 tbsp (15 ml) vanilla extract

2 cups (464 g) full-fat cream cheese, room temperature

2 cups (480 ml) full-fat sour cream, room temperature

⅓ cup (160 ml) browned honey, room temperature

To make the browned honey, place the honey in a large saucepan over medium heat. Cook until the temperature reads 248°F (120°C), or you can wait until it reads 266°F (130°C). It should take 5 to 7 minutes (the time may vary depending on the brand of honey). Stay close and constantly stir the honey, as it tends to boil over. Remove the pan from the heat and carefully drizzle in the cream while stirring.

Allow the honey to cool for about 1 hour, then transfer it into a glass container or jar. Store it at room temperature for 3 days or in the refrigerator for up to 10 days.

To make the cheesecake, preheat the oven to 425°F (218°C) and line one 8-inch (20-cm) round pan with parchment paper. Make sure the paper rises about 2 inches (5 cm) on all sides of the pan to protect the cake as it's puffing up during baking.

In a medium bowl, mix the sugar, flour and salt and stir to blend. Set aside. In a small measuring cup, mix together the egg yolks, eggs and vanilla. Set aside.

In the bowl of a stand mixer fitted with the paddle attachment, place the cream cheese and beat on low speed for about 2 minutes, until the cheese is smooth. Scrape the bottom and sides of the bowl. Add the sour cream and keep beating until the cream cheese and sour cream fully incorporate, about 2 more minutes. Stop the mixer and scrape the bottom and sides of the bowl.

With the mixer on low, add the sugar mixture and beat until fully incorporated, then slowly drizzle in the egg mixture. Stop the mixer and scrape the bottom and sides of the bowl. Pour the batter into the prepared pan, drizzle the browned honey on the batter, then use a knife or a toothpick to swirl the honey into the batter.

Bake for 38 to 45 minutes, until the cheesecake has puffed up and it jiggles in its center when you wiggle the pan. Remove the cheesecake from the oven and allow it to cool for 2 hours, then place it in the refrigerator to completely cool.

The cheesecake should be stored in the refrigerator, covered, for up to 3 days and served when completely cold.

NOTE

The steam that was trapped in the sides and bottom of the pan as the cheescake cools might turn back into liquids. It's okay and it doesn't affect the flavors or texture of the cheesecake.

Create Incredible Caramel Flavor

Caramel lovers, this science lesson and the following recipe are for you. These cupcakes are what caramel would taste like if transformed into a cupcake.

The cupcakes are soft, buttery and simply exploding with the color, smell and flavor of caramel. Even the silky smooth buttery caramel is an explosion of caramel flavors, and together they turn what we all know as cupcakes into a caramel lover's dream come true.

In the previous chapter (page 41), we talked about the properties of sugar (see page 58) and how, while it adds sweetness to our baked goods, it doesn't add any flavor unless caramelized.

During the caramelization process, the sugar molecules change their shape and transform from sweet, colorless, odorless molecules into dark molecules with an intense smell and rich, deep flavors.

The process of caramelization begins at 320°F (160°C). At that temperature, the sugar turns from colorless to a light golden brown and develops the sweet rich caramel flavor. As the temperature increases, the sugar turns darker and more bitter in a matter of seconds.

So, we need to find the best way to caramelize the sugar into a light golden color in order to achieve caramel flavors. This can be a fairly easy and simple process once we understand the science behind it and apply it.

When we caramelize sugar, we want the sugar to dissolve so the caramel has a smooth texture. However, sugar melts at 366°F (185°C), and at that temperature it's already very dark and bitter. So, when we cook sugar over the stove, some of the sugar melts and turns dark brown before the majority of it caramelizes, leaving us with a gritty and bitter caramel.

We prevent this by adding a small amount of water to the sugar to dissolve it (melt it) and allow the temperature to increase gradually. That way, when it turns golden, it will do so in an even way, preventing the sugar from being partly burnt and partly uncaramelized.

This is exactly what we do in the following recipe, creating a light golden caramel with a sweet deep flavor.

CARAMEL LOVER'S CUPCAKES

This recipe is a great example of the scientific reaction that creates caramel, which we use to infuse these cupcakes with caramel flavor!

YIELD: 15 cupcakes

CARAMEL MILK

1 cup (200 g) granulated sugar

¼ tsp cream of tartar

4 tbsp (60 ml) water

1 cup (240 ml) heavy cream, room temperature

1 cup (240 ml) milk, room temperature

CUPCAKES

2 cups (250 g) all-purpose flour

1 tsp baking powder

½ tsp salt

½ cup (114 g) unsalted butter, room temperature

¾ cup (150 g) granulated sugar

2 large eggs, room temperature

1 cup (240 ml) caramel milk, room temperature

To make the caramel milk, in a medium sauté pan, mix together the sugar and cream of tartar, then pour in the water and swirl the pan to make sure the sugar is coated with the water. Place the pan over medium heat until the mixture has turned a light golden color, 4 to 5 minutes. Stay close because once the sugar changes color, things happen very fast and the sugar can turn dark quickly. Don't stir the pan with a spoon or a spatula or the mixture will crystallize.

If you notice sugar crystals on the sides of the pan, gently dip a pastry brush in water and brush the sides of the pan. The sugar has yet to be caramelized and we want to prevent it from crystallizing (the opposite of a smooth caramel texture).

Once the sugar has turned golden, turn the heat off and pour in the cream and milk while stirring. You might notice some pieces of sugar candy, that's totally okay. Keep stirring until it's completely dissolved and the liquid becomes smooth. Pour the mixture into a large measuring cup and allow it to reach room temperature or refrigerate until ready to use.

To make the cupcakes, preheat the oven to 350°F (175°C) and line two cupcake pans with cupcakes liners. Set aside.

In a medium bowl, sift together the flour, baking powder and salt. Set aside.

In the bowl of a stand mixer fitted with the paddle attachment, beat the butter and sugar on medium-high speed until light and fluffy, 4 to 5 minutes. Add the eggs, one at a time, waiting for the egg to fully incorporate before adding the next. Scrape the bottom and sides of the bowl.

(continued)

CARAMEL LOVER'S CUPCAKES (cont.)

BUTTERCREAM

3 large egg yolks

2 tsp (5 g) cornstarch

1 cup (240 ml) caramel milk

1½ cups (341 g) unsalted butter, room temperature

⅓ cup (66 g) granulated sugar

CARAMEL TOPPING

¼ cup Caramel (Caramel-Filled Meringue Clouds [page 131])

Add the flour mixture in three additions, alternating with the caramel milk in two additions and making sure to start and finish with the flour mixture. Fill the cupcake liners two-thirds full and bake for 18 to 20 minutes, or until the tops of the cupcakes are light golden and a toothpick inserted into the center of the cupcakes comes out clean.

Remove the cupcakes from the oven and allow them to cool completely before frosting.

To make the buttercream, have a medium bowl and a sieve ready to use.

In the medium bowl, mix together the egg yolks and cornstarch until smooth. In a medium saucepan, heat the caramel milk. Once it starts to boil, slowly pour ½ cup (120 ml) of the caramel milk into the egg yolk mixture while stirring, then pour the egg yolk mixture into the remaining ½ cup (120 ml) of the caramel milk.

Cook on medium heat while constantly stirring, until the mixture starts to thicken and you notice large bubbles. Reduce the heat to low and cook for an additional 1 minute. Run the curd through a sieve into a clean bowl, cover the top with plastic wrap and allow it to cool to room temperature.

In a bowl of a stand mixer fitted with the paddle attachment, beat the butter and sugar on medium-high speed until light and fluffy, 5 to 7 minutes. Add the cooled curd and keep beating until the sugar has fully dissolved and the buttercream is smooth and fluffy, 8 to 10 minutes.

Fill a large piping bag fitted with a large star tip and pipe the cupcakes with the buttercream. Drizzle the cupcakes with the caramel topping.

The frosted cupcakes and buttercream can be stored at room temperature for up to 3 days.

Make Moist, Syrup-Soaked Cakes

Adding texture is the best way to elevate any dessert, like in the Maple Pecan Cake (page 97). The buttery, soft and tender cake is sprinkled with crunchy chopped pecans and layered with smooth and airy whipped cream. But the secret to turning this cake into a unique, moist and flavorful dessert is soaking it with cold maple syrup.

The rule for soaking a cake is pretty simple: The cake and the syrup have to be at opposite temperatures. Meaning, if the cake is warm, then the syrup should be cold or vice versa.

To better understand the reason for that, imagine that you're at your favorite band's live concert, 50 feet (15 m) from the stage, where naturally it's crowded with excited fans (Jamily, this one is for you!). You are dancing, having fun, not realizing that both you and your neighbors are bumping into each other, when you realize your drink is empty. The concession stand is about 150 feet (46 m) from where you are, and as you are trying to make your way toward it, you find that moving past the busy crowd isn't as simple as you would like it to be. Some people are dancing, jumping around, some are hugging or holding hands, and they're all standing in your way. But what if the same crowd would suddenly stop and have each person sit by themselves—how easy would it be for you to make your way to and back from the concession stand?

Well, in this example, the molecules in the cake are the excited fans, jumping, bumping, moving around, full of energy given by the warm temperature.

If both the cake and syrup are full of energy and moving around, like you and your fellow concertgoers, then the molecules will continue bumping into each other and, basically, getting nowhere.

In the same way, if both the cake and syrup are cold, then none of the molecules will have any energy to move at all. But if the cake is warm out of the oven and the syrup is cold straight out of the refrigerator, then we know that the cold syrup molecules that are lacking energy will make their way down the cake without any resistance as the warm cake molecules push and move them in every direction.

Now, it's true that the warm cake might naturally warm up the syrup, and this is why we need to make sure that the syrup is as cold as the cake is warm. So when you take the cake out of the oven, make sure the syrup has been cooling in the refrigerator for a while.

In the Maple Pecan Cake, we soak the hot, out-of-the-oven cake with the cold, out-of-the-refrigerator maple syrup.

And by doing that, we allow the molecules of the warm cake to bump into and push down the molecules of the cold syrup, which, due to the lack of energy, will not push back. The syrup molecules will find their way—or as close as possible—to the bottom of the cake, giving us a perfectly soaked, moist cake that's full of maple flavors in every. Single. Bite.

MAPLE PECAN CAKE

This recipe is a great example of how, by understanding the molecular properties of our baked goods, we can create even better textures for our treats.

YIELD: One 9 x 13–inch (23 x 33–cm) cake

CAKE

1 cup plus 2 tbsp (255 g) unsalted butter, room temperature

2 cups (250 g) all-purpose flour, divided

1½ cups (164 g) toasted chopped pecans, divided

2 tsp (9 g) baking powder

½ tsp salt

1 cup (120 ml) half-and-half, room temperature

1 tbsp (15 ml) vanilla extract

1 cup (200 g) granulated sugar

2 large eggs, room temperature

2 cups (480 ml) maple syrup, cold

Preheat the oven to 350°F (175°C). Grease a 2½ x 9 x 13–inch (6 x 23 x 33–cm) pan with 2 tablespoons (28 g) of butter, sprinkle with 4 tablespoons (32 g) of flour, then bang it over the sink to remove any excess flour. Set aside.

In a medium bowl, sift the remaining 1¾ cups (219 g) of flour. Place ½ cup (55 g) of pecans in a food processor, sprinkle with 2 tablespoons (16 g) of the sifted flour, then process until the mixture is a very fine texture. Add the processed pecans to the sifted flour, mix in the baking powder and salt, and use a fork to fully incorporate the ingredients.

In a large measuring cup, measure the half-and-half and stir in the vanilla. Set aside.

In the bowl of a stand mixer fitted with the paddle attachment, beat the remaining butter and sugar on medium-high speed until light in color and fluffy, 4 to 5 minutes. Scrape the bottom and sides of the bowl. Add the eggs, one at a time, waiting for each egg to fully incorporate before adding the next.

Add the flour mixture in three additions, alternating with the half-and-half, making sure to start and finish with the flour mixture.

Once you add the last portion of the flour, stop the mixer, add the remaining 1 cup (109 g) of pecans and use a rubber spatula to incorporate the pecans and any flour residue.

Spread the batter into the prepared pan and bake for 30 to 35 minutes on the middle rack. It's ready when a toothpick inserted into the center of the cake comes out clean and the top is lightly golden.

(continued)

MAPLE PECAN
CAKE (cont.)

WHIPPED CREAM

2 tsp (2 g) gelatin

1 tbsp (15 ml) water

2 cups (480 ml) heavy cream

2 tbsp (30 g) granulated sugar

⅓ cup (36 g) toasted chopped pecans

Remove the cake from the oven and immediately pour the cold maple syrup on top. Allow the cake to soak up the syrup and cool before topping it with whipped cream.

To make the whipped cream, in a small bowl, place the gelatin and mix in the water. Allow for the gelatin to bloom for 3 to 4 minutes. Warm the bloomed gelatin in the microwave for 4 to 5 seconds.

In the bowl of a stand mixer fitted with the whisk attachment, pour the cream, add the sugar and whip on low. Once you notice the cream is starting to thicken, gradually increase the speed to medium-high. When you notice that the cream is thick, add the melted gelatin and increase the speed to high. Whip until the cream is thick and stabilized.

Once the cake is cooled, spread the whipped cream and sprinkle with the pecans. The cake is best served at room temperature and, once frosted, should be refrigerated within 3 hours.

NOTES

Make sure that the gelatin is not warmer than room temperature when adding it to the cream, otherwise it will clump and won't get distributed.

You can substitute 1 cup (240 ml) of maple syrup with an equal amount of cold milk.

How to Bake Flawless Madeleines

These beautifully shaped madeleines are tiny, tender moist cakes loaded with unique pistachio and orange blossom flavors. What makes madeleines so extraordinary is their special shape and texture, which is accomplished by the manipulation of temperature.

Madeleine cookies are made using the sponge cake formula (see page 119), but unlike a traditional sponge cake—which is light, airy and rises evenly at the top—madeleine cookies are relatively dense and have a distinct hump at the top.

This is achieved by taking the time to cool the batter twice: once when we're finished with the mixing process and again after we divide the batter in the molds.

Let's get into the science behind it.

During the first cooling process, we allow the starches in the flour to absorb as much liquid as possible, and as a result, they lower the amount of free moisture (meaning any liquid that's between the molecules) in the batter.

Next, it's time to fill the molds with batter three-quarters full and place them back in the refrigerator. The cold temperature in the refrigerator, coupled with the fact that we lowered the moisture in the batter during the first cooling process, will help us create a thin dry layer at the top of each madeleine.

When we bake the madeleines, this thin dry top will make it hard for the steam to escape evenly from the sides of the cookies. So instead, the steam makes its way to the center, forming a beautiful hump at the center of each madeleine.

The oven's high temperature of 400°F (205°C) also has a role in the shaping of the madeleines. The high temperature will apply enough energy to further dry the top of the cookies and also to fully set and bake them before the steam finds its way out. As we know, steam is water that went through a state transition and turned into gas. The good news is that the trapped steam turns back into water as the cookies cool, providing extra moisture to the madeleines.

One extra step we can take to truly add flavor and texture to our madeleines is with the help of our molds. As you'll see, the first step is to brush the molds with melted butter and sprinkle them with flour. This is important because the flour will soak up all of the water from the butter, leaving us with fat and milk solids. As we bake, the Maillard reaction (page 88) will create a beautiful, delicious and crisp brown layer.

The Pistachio–Orange Blossom Madeleines recipe (page 102) calls for using the sponge cake mixing method, as well as the two-step cooling process mentioned above. As a result, the cookies are light and tender—because we incorporated so many air bubbles during the mixing process—as well as moist due to the steam that was trapped and could not escape because we took the time to cool and dry the tops of the cookies, which is also why the cookies have the beautiful "hump" they're so famous for.

And that extra step of greasing and cooling the pan gives the cookies such a beautiful golden dark color that intensifies the flavors.

PISTACHIO-ORANGE BLOSSOM MADELEINES

This recipe is a great example of how we can manipulate temperature to create elevated treats like madeleines.

YIELD: 12 medium-sized madeleines

10 tbsp (140 g) unsalted butter, melted, divided

2 tbsp (16 g) all-purpose flour, for greasing the molds

½ cup (50 g) chopped roasted pistachios

¾ cup plus 1 tbsp (100 g) cake flour, divided

½ tsp baking powder

2 large eggs, room temperature

½ cup (100 g) granulated sugar

2 tsp (10 ml) orange blossom water

Using a pastry brush, brush the molds with 2 tablespoons (28 g) of melted butter, then sprinkle them with the all-purpose flour. Shake to fully distribute the mixture, then turn them over and bang out any excess flour over the sink. Place the molds in the refrigerator.

In a food processor, place the chopped pistachios and 1 tablespoon (8 g) of cake flour and process until it resembles a fine meal.

In a medium bowl, sift the remaining ¾ cup (90 g) of cake flour and baking powder, then add the processed pistachios and use a fork to incorporate. Set aside.

In the bowl of a stand mixer fitted with the whisk attachment, place the eggs and sugar and mix on high speed until very light in color, 3 to 4 minutes.

Sift the flour mixture over the egg mixture, then use a rubber spatula to gently fold the flour into the eggs. Once fully incorporated, drizzle in the remaining melted butter and orange blossom water and fold to fully incorporate.

Place the bowl in the refrigerator for 30 minutes.

Remove the batter from the refrigerator and fill the molds three-quarters full. Place them back in the refrigerator to cool for a minimum of 1 hour or a maximum of 4 hours.

When ready to bake, preheat the oven to 400°F (205°C) and place the molds on the middle rack. Bake for 8 to 10 minutes, turning the pans at the 6-minute mark. The madeleines are ready when the centers look dry and have risen to humps and a toothpick inserted into the center of the cookies comes out clean.

Remove the cookies from the oven and let them cool for 5 to 10 minutes before removing them from the molds.

*See image on previous page.

How to Enhance Chocolate Flavor

If you wonder whether the world needs yet another chocolate cupcake recipe, the answer is YES! Especially one that fills your kitchen with an intense aroma and your belly with soft, tender cupcakes that are loaded with amazing and complex chocolate flavors and have distinguished and impressive glossy tops.

The key to the flavors and attractive appearance of these cupcakes is the simple act of blooming the cocoa powder.

The verb "blooming" is quite common in the baking world, and it refers to the chemical reaction of a dry substance in the presence of liquid—for example, dry gelatin molecules swell when dissolved in water. "Blooming" cocoa powder means pouring a hot liquid over the cocoa powder. But unlike other substances such as gelatin and flour, the cocoa powder isn't a thickening agent. Its great contribution is to the flavor and appearance of our baked goods.

So what is chocolate blooming and why do we do that?

To better understand, let's explain the science behind it, starting with where the term "blooming" comes from. When we bite into a piece of chocolate, what gives it a firm texture and a shiny appearance is the cocoa butter that has crystallized by perfectly aligning six different forms of crystals.

Imagine a perfectly square Lego® puzzle, made of different sizes of Lego pieces.

Each crystal has a different name, texture and firmness. The crystal that's responsible for the shiny appearance and snappy texture of chocolate is called beta. It's the most stable crystal, and for that crystal to stay stable and aligned perfectly with other types of crystals, the chocolate needs to be cooled to a temperature of 34°F (1°C), then stored at a temperature of 60 to 65°F (15 to 18°C).

If the chocolate is stored at a higher temperature, then the alignment of the crystals will be unstable. Those unstable crystals will make their way to the beta crystals and form a large coarse fat that will migrate to the surface of the chocolate and appear to our eyes as an unpleasant white powder. This process is referred to as "fat bloom," and we see it plenty on the surface of old chocolate bars or when a melted chocolate has cooled down without the proper tempering.

So now we know how sensitive chocolate is to temperature. The same is true for cocoa powder. Cocoa powder contains, by United States law, 10 percent fat. The average percent of fat found in a commercial U.S. cocoa powder brand is 10 to 12 percent fat and a European brand is 20 to 22 percent fat, as well as 20 to 25 percent starch and sugar. Much like the migration of fat in the process of "fat bloom" we explored in this section, when we pour hot liquid on top of cocoa powder, the warm temperature will disrupt the structure of the fat molecules. As a result, those molecules migrate to the surface, causing an increase in flavor, a strong aroma and a pleasant shiny appearance. That means that in addition to flavor, blooming chocolate helps with the appearance of our baked goods.

(continued)

HOW TO ENHANCE CHOCOLATE FLAVOR (cont.)

What gives these Simple-Yet-Fabulous Chocolate Cupcakes (page 106) such a strong chocolate flavor is the fact that we take the time to bloom the cocoa powder. The very first step calls for measuring the cocoa powder, then for blooming it by pouring boiling coffee over it. (If you are wondering why coffee, it's because coffee enhances chocolate flavors.)

Once we pour the coffee and mix it in, we can instantly smell the strong chocolate aroma and see a thin shiny layer at the surface.

At this point, we'll allow the mixture to sit, bloom and eventually cool to room temperature while we measure and mix the remaining ingredients. Adding the cocoa mixture last is a way to make sure our ingredients are all at the same temperature when we mix them together.

And finally, as we take the cupcakes out of the oven and allow them to cool, we can clearly notice a beautiful shiny top accompanied by strong and delicious chocolate flavors.

You can top the cupcakes with Chocolate Ganache (page 150), Old-Fashioned Buttercream (page 32) or your favorite frosting.

SIMPLE-YET-FABULOUS CHOCOLATE CUPCAKES

This recipe is a great example of the science behind chocolate blooming and why it boosts chocolate flavor.

YIELD: 12 cupcakes

½ cup (44 g) unsweetened cocoa powder

¾ cup (180 ml) boiling coffee

½ cup (120 ml) milk, room temperature

1 tbsp (15 ml) vanilla extract

1 large egg, room temperature

2 large egg yolks, room temperature

1¾ cups (210 g) cake flour

1 tsp baking powder

¼ tsp baking soda

1 cup (200 g) granulated sugar

½ cup (114 g) unsalted butter, room temperature (cut into ½-inch [1.3-cm] pieces)

FROSTING OPTIONS
Old Fashioned Chocolate Buttercream (page 32)
Chocolate Ganache (page 150)

Preheat the oven to 350°F (175°C) and line one 12-cavity cupcake pan with cupcake liners.

In a medium bowl, measure and bloom the cocoa powder by pouring the boiling coffee over it. Stir until smooth, then set aside.

In a measuring cup, mix the milk, vanilla, egg and egg yolks. Set aside.

In the bowl of a stand mixer, sift the flour, baking powder and baking soda. Stir in the sugar and beat on low speed using the paddle attachment. Increase the mixer speed to medium and add the butter. Beat until the flour mixture resembles a coarse meal.

Pour in the milk mixture, increase the mixer speed to medium-high and beat for about 20 seconds. The milk mixture should be fully incorporated and the flour mixture should be mostly smooth. Reduce the mixer speed to medium-low and pour in the cocoa mixture. Then, increase the speed to medium-high and beat until the mixture is smooth, 20 to 25 seconds, stopping the mixer halfway to scrape the bottom and sides of the bowl. Stop the mixer and let the batter rest for 10 minutes.

Using a cookie scoop, fill the cupcake liners two-thirds full and bake them on the middle rack for 20 minutes. The cupcakes are ready when a round mound has formed on top and is dry to the touch of your finger, and a toothpick inserted into the center of the cupcakes comes out clean.

Remove the cupcakes from the oven and allow them to completely cool before frosting and/or filling.

The cupcakes are best eaten within 36 hours and can be stored in the freezer for up to 3 weeks.

*See image on previous page.

Bake Perfectly Round Cookies

The best thing about the Classic Peanut Butter Cookies (page 110) is that they taste like peanut butter. But they don't stick to the roof of your mouth, so we get extra space to reach for some more cookies—before they're claimed and gone! These cookies can be enjoyed as is or filled with jelly—or even any type of ganache (see the Chocolate Ganache recipe on page 150).

The peanut butter gives these cookies an incredible flavor; the cookies get their crumbly and crispy-yet-tender texture from the addition of ground peanuts and ground oats. But their chubby figures and perfectly symmetrical shapes come from understanding how to use fat's melting point to get the perfectly round shape that we aspire to in cookies!

When we bake, it's hard to fully predict the baked size, shape and texture of the raw dough or batter. That's especially true when it comes to cookies. I'm always amazed by how firm cookie dough that doesn't even stick to my hands can spread and take over more than one-fourth of the baking pan.

Since we bake cookies on a flat sheet—rather than in a cake mold or loaf pan—the steam and gas they produce while baking (pages 70 to 75) is allowed to spread sideways, not just upward.

So how can we prevent our cookies from spreading, preserving their "chubby" round figure?

One way is to decrease the amount of water that's in the dough, since that will decrease the amount of steam—but that means decreasing the number of eggs, which also help the cookies firm and spread less—or by reducing the amount of sugar, which gives the cookies their sweet flavor. Neither are ideal options!

There is one more ingredient that contributes to the spreading of cookies—fat.

When we place cookies (or any other baked goods) in the oven, there's a lot going on: sugar dissolves, gas and steam form and expand, eggs' and starches' proteins coagulate and the fat melts, turning into liquid. As the fat melts and turns into liquid, it moves only one way: sideways.

(continued)

BAKE PERFECTLY ROUND COOKIES (cont.)

If we give the proteins and starches a chance to coagulate (bond) and to set before the fat melts, then the cookies will spread less. To accomplish this, we'll have to understand the temperatures that these reactions all happen at.

Egg and gluten proteins start to coagulate and firm our baked goods at 140 to 160°F (60 to 70°C). Starches coagulate at 120 to 140°F (49 to 60°C).

Butter starts to melt at 90 to 95°F (32 to 35°C), but vegetable shortening's melting point is 117°F (47°C). That's a significant difference, and the secret to forming perfectly round cookies!

As we can see on page 86, our recipes bake from the edges toward the inside, since the edges are the first to receive heat/energy. This means that the cookies will reach the necessary coagulation temperature on the top and sides of the cookie first.

Since a significant amount of vegetable shortening needs to melt in order for it to considerably spread the cookies—and it has a higher melting point than butter—the tops and sides of the cookies have the chance to coagulate before the vegetable shortening reaches its melting point, stopping the cookie dough spreading and preserving the ideal round cookie shape!

NOTE

While using vegetable shortening prevents the cookies from spreading significantly, it doesn't eliminate the spreading completely because there are other elements that might affect the baking process, such as the oven's temperature, the size of the cookies, etc. However, it's a great scientific way to use the melting point to our advantage.

CLASSIC PEANUT BUTTER COOKIES

This recipe is a great example of how to use what we know about fat's melting point to shape your cookies.

YIELD: 18–24 cookies

¾ cup (68 g) uncooked rolled oats

¾ cup (110 g) unsalted roasted peanuts

⅓ cup (70 g) vegetable shortening

½ cup plus 2 tbsp (120 g) granulated sugar

1 cup (258 g) smooth peanut butter

1 large egg

½ tsp salt

Preheat the oven to 350°F (175°C) and line two 13 x 18–inch (33 x 45–cm) half-sheet cookie pans with parchment paper.

In a food processor, process the oats into a fine meal. Add the peanuts and process until they're very fine. Place the oat-peanut mixture in a medium bowl and set aside.

In the bowl of a stand mixer, place the shortening, sugar, peanut butter, egg and salt and mix on medium-high speed until a smooth mixture forms. Add the oat-peanut mixture and mix to combine.

Using a medium cookie spoon (holds 1½ tablespoons [22 g]), scoop the cookie dough and place it on the pans, leaving 1½ inches (4 cm) of space between the cookies. Using the back of a fork, mark each cookie horizontally and then vertically.

Bake for 15 to 18 minutes, or until the cookies are golden on the sides. The cookies are ready when they're slightly puffed at the center and the bottom edges are lightly browned.

The cookies should be stored covered at room temperature for up to 10 days.

* See image on previous page.

Is Freezing a Form of Baking?

The Strawberry Shortcake Popsicles (page 113) are a sweet, creamy and refreshing way to enjoy strawberry shortcake on a stick. And even though we don't use the oven at all, this recipe can still be considered baking!

When we bake, we don't just place certain amounts of ingredients in a bowl and wait for them to magically turn into cakes, cookies, pies, etc. Whether we know it or not, we're actually using chemical, physical, or even biological reactions to create different flavors and textures.

As long as one of these types of reactions happens—and results in a change of flavor or texture—we can refer to it as baking. Therefore, freezing is a type of baking!

The popsicles recipe is a wonderful example of how we can use molecules' reactions to temperature to combine separate ingredients. The recipe does this in two stages: Stage one uses heat and stage two uses the opposite of heat—freezing.

The heat is firstly and mainly used to create flavors. The dried milk powder contains both sugar and protein, and as we heat it, the Maillard reaction (page 88) occurs, giving us a rich, complex and delicious flavor. Then we cook the strawberries, allowing the heat to extract flavors from them as well.

Heat also helps with texture; it melts the butter and makes it go through a physical state transition from solid to liquid. Then, the butter coats the strawberries—giving us a smooth and flavorful texture. The cornstarch is absorbing the liquids, making the mixture thick and full. And when we mix all of these components together, we have a strong, sweet and unbelievably delicious mixture that resembles strawberry shortcake.

In the last step, we'll freeze the mixture, using temperature to make our thick-yet-liquid mixture undergo a state transition and turn from liquid into solid.

As mentioned in the chapter introduction, temperature is a quantifiable number to demonstrate the amount of energy—or lack of energy. Water is liquid at 75°F (24°C), meaning the water molecules have enough energy to move around and stay liquid, but at a temperature of 32°F (0°C), the molecules have no energy to move, so they get as close to each other as they can. That gives us ice.

This state-transition process is a physical reaction, and we'll use it when we place the mixture into popsicle molds and allow the low temperature of the freezer to stop any molecular activity. The molecules huddle close together, giving us firm, delicious and refreshing strawberry popsicles.

NOTE

Even though the popsicles' mixture contains a lot of water, it will not freeze at 32°F (0°C). Other ingredients in the mixture, such as sugar, heavy cream and sweetened condensed milk, have a lower freezing point, which lowers the overall freezing temperature of the mixture. In fact, this is why most home freezers average 0°F (-18°C).

STRAWBERRY SHORTCAKE POPSICLES

This recipe is a great example of the power of phase transitions.

YIELD: 5 popsicles

---

1 tbsp (7 g) dried milk powder

¾ cup (180 ml) heavy cream, divided

2 tbsp (28 g) unsalted butter

2 cups (332 g) fresh strawberries (sliced into ½-inch [1.3-cm] pieces)

2 tbsp (16 g) cornstarch

1 tbsp (15 ml) water

½ cup (120 ml) sweetened condensed milk

In a small pan over medium-low heat, place the milk powder and heat it until brown, stirring constantly, for 2 to 3 minutes.

Add ¼ cup (60 ml) of cream on top of the browned milk powder and mix to distribute. Then pour in the remaining ½ cup (120 ml) of the cream. Set aside.

In a large sauté pan, melt the butter, then add the strawberries and cook on medium heat until the strawberries are soft, about 15 minutes.

In a small bowl, mix together the cornstarch and water, pour it over the cream, then pour the cream over the strawberries. Using a wooden spoon, stir and cook on low heat, until the mixture is starting to thicken, about 2 minutes. Remove from the heat and let cool for 5 minutes.

Pour the sweetened condensed milk over the strawberries and mix to fully incorporate.

Pour the mixture into popsicle molds and freeze them for a minimum of 6 hours or for up to 3 weeks.

NOTE

I like to run a popsicle under tap water for 2 seconds before eating it. This way, the temperature of the popsicle's exterior goes down, giving it a more pleasant texture and bringing some flavors to the surface.

FOOLPROOF FORMULAS:
The Easy, Scientific Way to Assure Your Baked Goods Succeed

Flour, sugar, butter, eggs and leavening agents are the most common ingredients in baking—and each has an important role in the complex and delicate process. Baking begins with the decision to roll up our sleeves and start creating. The next steps involve counting eggs, measuring sugar and butter, sifting flour and leavening agents, followed by the mixing process and, lastly, baking.

We don't use the same amount of ingredients or the same mixing method each time we bake. For different baked goods, we use a different recipe or, as I like to call it, a baking formula—a list of ingredients followed by the method. These baking formulas call for an exact measurement of the ingredients and even the smallest change can affect the quality of the baked goods.

In this chapter, I'm sharing foolproof formulas for all your favorite baked goods. We'll learn how to create all sorts of baked goods, a tender and moist cake (page 119), crumbly cookies (page 144), creamy custard (page 151) and even a flaky and buttery piecrust (page 140). We'll cover which ingredients to use, how much and how to incorporate them for best results. And by the end of this chapter, you'll have the tools and knowledge to develop your very own foolproof formulas.

What makes a foolproof formula and how do we go about it?

Each formula is made up of a specific amount of ingredients and a specific way of combining them—in scientific terms, a ratio and a mixing method.

A ratio is a fixed proportion of an ingredient relative to the other ingredients in the formula. The ratios in this chapter are presented as the "baker's percentage." With the baker's percentage, an ingredient (most often the flour), is expressed as 100 percent, and each other ingredient is expressed as a percentage relative to it. For example, if I have 1 cup (125 g) of flour and the ratio I'm using calls for flour 100 percent and sugar 50 percent, then according to the ratio, the granulated sugar is 50 percent of the amount of flour. So for this recipe, I'd be using 1 cup (125 g) of flour and a bit more than ¼ cup (63 g) of granulated sugar in my baking!

The mixing method, the way we incorporate the ingredients, is the second important part of the baking formula. It can be the difference between a dense and rich pound cake and light and airy sponge cupcake, even when we use the exact same amount of ingredients. Cakes—whether pound cakes, angel food cakes or butter cakes—all get their melt-in-your-mouth, tender texture from the air bubbles we incorporate during the mixing process, in a process called aeration (page 45). The method by which we incorporate the air into the batter is the reason different cakes have such a different texture and appearance.

Pound cakes and sponge cakes are excellent examples of the importance of the mixing method. Both recipes call for the same ratio of ingredients, but the mixing process is very different and results in two different cakes. While a pound cake is dense and moist, a sponge cake is light and airy.

So, in fact, you can use any pound cake recipe and convert it into a sponge cake by changing the mixing methods.

Rich Pound and Butter Cakes

Pound cakes are rich, tall and usually baked in Bundt pans. Butter cakes, having lower amounts of fat and eggs, are great for making layer cakes or snack (coffee) cakes. Get ready to create moist, indulgent pound and butter cakes every time by following this foolproof formula. Once you've perfected it, you can start using this ratio and mixing method to create your own recipes!

Pound Cake Ratio:
Flour 100%; Fat 100%; Sugar 100%; Eggs 100%

Butter Cake Ratio:
Flour 100%; Fat 45%; Sugar 100%; Eggs 40%

As you can see, the pound cake and butter cake ratios don't mention any addition of liquids. And even though we can bake the cakes without any, the addition of liquids adds flavor, moisture and more structure (see the Orange Cream Cheese Cake recipe on page 15).

So that leaves us with the question of how much liquid to add. Well, there's no specific answer. It's a game of trial and error, and it might require making adjustments to the other ingredients. I recommend starting with half the amount of flour and proceeding from there.

Mixing Method

Pound cakes and butter cakes are made using the creaming method and/or the two-stages method.

The Almond-Chocolate Pound Cake (page 118) is a great example of a traditional pound cake using the creaming method. We begin by creaming the fat, whether it's butter or shortening, with the sugar. The sugar creates tiny holes in the butter that are filled with air and later, during baking, those tiny air bubbles expand and bring volume and height to the cake, as well as texture.

Next is adding the eggs, one egg at a time. Eggs provide protein, fat and water, and as we know, water doesn't mix with fat. It's true that as the eggs are mixed into the batter, they will also emulsify and allow the fat and water to incorporate (page 22). But if we add the eggs all at once, the emulsification will break and the mixture will curdle and deflate.

Once the eggs have been fully incorporated, we can mix in the dry ingredients in three stages, to help the mixture absorb the dry ingredients properly. If a recipe calls for any liquid ingredients, then we add the liquids in two additions, alternating with the dry ingredients, making sure to start and end with the dry ingredients.

The process is simple and straightforward, but it takes all of the above steps to achieve a tender and moist pound or butter cake.

The Two-Stages Method

The two-stages method, or the two-stage method, is a very simple method bakers love using, especially when using the butter ratio for layered cakes or cupcakes. You can find an example of this method on pages 162 and 164. In this method, we aerate the dry ingredients, sugar and fat together by mixing them with a paddle attachment or hand mixer until the flour is fully coated with the fat and the mixture resembles wet sand. Then, we add the eggs and liquids together and mix them into a cohesive batter. And that's it.

I can't think of anything more comforting than a buttery, moist and tender pound cake, like the Almond-Chocolate Pound Cake (page 118). As you bite into the cake, a burst of a buttery and rich almond flavor melts in your mouth, followed by a "kick" of chocolate—adding even more deliciousness.

ALMOND–CHOCOLATE POUND CAKE

This recipe is a great example of the pound cake ratio and mixing method.

YIELD: One 2½ x 4 x 9–inch (6 x 10 x 23–cm) cake

Baker's spray for greasing the pan

¾ cup plus 1 tbsp (184 g) unsalted butter, room temperature

1½ cups (188 g) all-purpose flour, plus more for pan

1 tsp baking powder

½ tsp salt

½ cup (120 ml) full-fat milk, room temperature

1 tsp almond extract

1 tsp vanilla extract

1 cup (200 g) granulated sugar

3 tbsp (45 g) almond paste

3 large eggs, room temperature

⅓ cup (45 g) semisweet chocolate, melted

Preheat the oven to 350°F (175°C), grease the bottom and sides of one 2½ x 4 x 9–inch (6 x 10 x 23–cm) loaf pan with baker's spray, then line the pan with parchment paper.

In a medium bowl, sift the flour, baking powder and salt and mix to blend. Set aside. In a measuring cup, mix the milk, almond extract and vanilla. Set aside.

In the bowl of a stand mixer fitted with the paddle attachment, beat the butter, sugar and almond paste together on medium-high speed until the mixture is light and fluffy, about 5 minutes. This step is what aerates the cake and gives it the ideal light and fluffy texture. Be sure to scrape the bottom and sides of the bowl a few times during this process. Sometimes, the paddle doesn't reach the bottom and sides of the bowl, which means some of the mixture doesn't get aerated.

Add the eggs, one at a time, waiting for each egg to fully incorporate before adding the next. Scrape the bottom and sides of the bowl to allow a full blending of the mixture. Add the flour mixture in three additions, alternating with the milk mixture, making sure to start and end with the flour.

Once you add the last portion of the flour mixture, turn the mixer off and use a rubber spatula to fully incorporate the flour.

Evenly spread the batter into the prepared pan, then pour the melted chocolate on top of the cake. Use a knife or a wooden skewer to gently incorporate the chocolate into the batter by swirling.

Bake for 35 to 40 minutes, or until the top of the cake appears dry and a toothpick inserted into the center of the cake comes out clean. Remove the cake from the oven and allow it to cool for 10 minutes before inverting it to serve.

The cake can be stored covered at room temperature for up to 3 days or frozen for up to 1 month.

*See image on previous page.

Tender, Crumbly Sponge Cake

Sponge cakes are so diverse. We can create all sorts of fun recipes once we learn the ratio and mixing method, like genoises, ladyfingers and even madeleines. It's with great intention that I placed the sponge cake ratio and mixing method right after the pound cake.

As you can see below, sponge cakes and pound cakes have the exact same ratio, but they have complete opposite textures. While pound cakes are dense and rich, sponge cakes are light, airy and fluffy. What causes the change is the mixing method. In sponge cakes, we incorporate air in the eggs, allowing the batter to increase its volume by three times, a much higher proportion than in pound cakes.

Sponge Cake Ratio:
Flour 100%; Fat 0–100%;
Sugar 100%; Eggs 100%

Mixing Method

The sponge cake method, also known as the whipping method, begins by whipping aerated whole room-temperature eggs, or egg yolks, with sugar until the mixture is light, thick and has tripled in size.

Dry ingredients are then folded in followed by the fat (if using).

Sponge cakes tend to rise very high and have a light and tender texture due to their long aeration process.

There are two key points when making sponge cake batter: first is the temperature of the eggs. The egg yolk's protein is a lot more stable than the protein of the egg whites, so it requires heat (or energy) to unfold, coagulate and trap the air. That's why we need our eggs to be at least at room temperature.

This is why many bakers take an extra step and whip the eggs and sugar over a double boiler to ensure a maximum capacity of air bubbles.

The second key point is the way we incorporate the dry ingredients and fat. Make sure to fold—not mix—in the ingredients. When we fold instead of mix, we incorporate the ingredients without deflating the air bubbles we worked so hard to incorporate.

In the Strawberry-Peach Sponge Cupcakes recipe (page 121), we take the extra step of sifting the cake flour three times, not only to aerate the flour but also to eliminate any flour clumps we might not notice.

These tender and light cupcakes are a refreshing summer (or any season) treat. They absorb the sweet fruit syrup easily, and along with the firm fruits and smooth whipped cream frosting, we have a beautiful and invigorating composition of flavors and textures.

STRAWBERRY–PEACH SPONGE CUPCAKES

This recipe is a great example of the sponge cake ratio and mixing method.

YIELD: 12 cupcakes

CUPCAKES

1¼ cups (150 g) cake flour

3 large eggs, room temperature

¾ cup (150 g) granulated sugar

⅔ cup (160 ml) vegetable oil or melted and cooled unsalted butter

WHIPPED CREAM

¼ cup (50 g) granulated sugar

¼ tsp xanthan gum

1 cup (240 ml) heavy cream

FILLING AND SYRUP

½ cup (83 g) chopped strawberries

1 cup (100 g) chopped canned peaches

½ cup (120 ml) canned peaches syrup

¼ cup (27 g) toasted slivered almonds

Preheat the oven to 350°F (175°C) and line a cupcake pan with cupcake liners. Set aside.

In a large bowl, sift the flour three times. Set aside.

In the bowl of a stand mixer, beat the eggs and sugar, starting on a low speed and gradually increasing to high. Keep beating until the mixture is pale yellow and has tripled in size, 4 to 5 minutes. Stop the mixer and gently fold in the flour. Drizzle in the oil or melted butter once the flour fully incorporates and fold until blended.

Fill the cupcake liners three-fourths full and bake for 12 to 13 minutes. The cupcakes are done when the tops are light golden and a toothpick inserted into the centers of the cupcakes comes out clean.

Remove the cupcakes from the oven and allow them to cool completely before filling and topping.

To make the whipped cream, mix the sugar with xanthan gum in a small bowl. Add it to the cream, then beat the mixture on high until thickened, 2 to 3 minutes. Fill a large piping bag fitted with a large star tip.

To make the filling and syrup, in a medium bowl, mix together the strawberries and peaches.

In a microwave or a saucepan, heat the peach syrup. Using a knife, gently cut a 1-inch (2.5-cm) dent out from the center of each cupcake. You can enjoy the leftovers as a snack or as crumbs to sprinkle on top of the cupcakes.

Using a pastry brush or a spoon, soak each cupcake with 1 teaspoon of peach syrup, then fill the holes you made in the cupcakes with the strawberry-peach mixture, reserving a few pieces of fruit to top the cupcake. Pipe the cupcakes with whipped cream and sprinkle them with chopped fruit, almonds and cupcake crumbs, if desired.

The cupcakes are best eaten at room temperature and need to be refrigerated within 4 hours of piping. They can be stored in the refrigerator for up to 3 days.

Melt-in-Your-Mouth Chiffon Cake

Including the chiffon cake ratio and mixing method was a must because chiffon cakes are the best! They are light, tender and moist—and I like to think of chiffon cakes as being the child of sponge cake and angel food cake. They're tall and light, much like an angel food cake, while also tender and crumbly like a sponge cake. We can see and taste the tiny air bubbles, with their melt-in-your-mouth texture.

Having liquid as part of the ratio gives us unlimited opportunities to incorporate flavor. In my Orange Chiffon Cake recipe (page 124), we added some orange juice and zest, which provides the cake with a refreshing and wonderful flavor. Because the chiffon cake is aerated with meringue, each bite is a citrus heaven.

Chiffon Cake Ratio:
Flour 100%; Eggs 100–200%;
Fat 50%; Sugar 100%; Liquid 50%

Chiffon cake is interesting because its ratio has its very own ratio of eggs, with two parts egg whites and one part egg yolk. This ratio is key to the success of the cake. If we use the same amount of egg yolks, the cake will be too heavy, and instead of rising high and tall, it will turn out dense and short.

Mixing Method

When we bake chiffon cake, we mix together the egg yolk and liquids, then mix in the sifted dry ingredients (flour, baking powder and salt). Separately, we create soft meringue with the egg whites and part of the sugar, which we then fold into the egg yolk and flour mixture.

There are a lot of similarities between angel food cake and chiffon cake. First is that just like we want to avoid over-whipping the egg whites when we bake angel food cake, we shouldn't whip the egg whites beyond a soft-medium peak (page 129) when baking a chiffon cake. Otherwise, the meringue will trap the water too tightly and prevent it from steaming and expanding the cake (see page 26 for more information).

Another similarity is that both cakes are baked in an angel food tube pan and cooled upside down in order to maintain their impressive heights and light textures.

ORANGE CHIFFON CAKE

This recipe is a great example of the chiffon cake ratio and mixing method.

YIELD: One 9 x 4–inch (23 x 10 x 23–cm) cake

7 egg yolks

⅔ cup (160 ml) fresh-squeezed orange juice

⅔ cup (160 ml) vegetable oil

Zest of 1 medium orange

2½ cups (300 g) cake flour

2 tsp (9 g) baking powder

½ tsp salt

1½ cups (300 g) granulated sugar, divided

7 egg whites

⅛ tsp cream of tartar

Preheat the oven to 325°F (160°C). Set aside a 9 x 4–inch (23 x 10–cm) angel food pan with feet. Don't grease the pan.

In a large bowl, whisk together the egg yolks, orange juice, oil and orange zest.

In a medium bowl, sift together the cake flour, baking powder, salt and 1 cup (200 g) of sugar. Use a fork to blend, then mix the flour mixture with the egg yolk mixture and whisk them together just until combined. Make sure not to over-beat or the cake will turn out too stiff.

In a separate bowl, place the egg whites and cream of tartar. Use a hand mixer (or a stand mixer) to whip the egg whites until frothy, 1 to 2 minutes.

Gradually add the remaining ½ cup (100 g) of sugar and whip until a firm (but not stiff) meringue has formed, 2 to 3 minutes. Depending on the strength of your mixer, it would be wise to stay put. Gently fold the meringue into the yolk and flour mixture.

Pour the mixture into the pan, gently tap the pan once on the counter, then place it on the middle rack. Bake for 50 to 60 minutes, or until the top of the cake is golden brown and springs back and a toothpick inserted into the center of the cake comes out clean.

Immediately upon taking the cake out of the oven, turn it upside down with the feet on the counter, allowing a minimum of 1 inch (2.5 cm) of space between the cake and the counter. (If your pan doesn't have feet, simply insert a bottle with a narrow neck into the center of the pan and allow the pan to rest upside down.)

The cake can be stored covered at room temperature for up to 3 days.

*See image on the previous page.

Airy Angel Food Cake

The absence of fat makes angel food cakes the lightest and airiest of them all—and the Strawberry Angel Food Cake recipe (page 127) is no exception. Angel food cakes are full of tiny air bubbles we can easily see once we cut into the cake. The light and airy texture of the cake goes wonderfully with whipped cream, and the sweet strawberry flavor of my recipe goes perfectly with bananas, nuts or even more strawberries.

Angel food cakes rise high and are so light. They're cooled upside down without any concern that the cake might deflate as it cools down.

**Angel Food Cake Ratio: Flour 100%;
Egg Whites 300%; Sugar 250–300%**

Mixing Method

Making angel food cake only requires three ingredients and the aeration of a large amount of egg whites. The egg whites should not be whipped beyond soft-medium peaks—or else the protein will trap the water too tightly and prevent it from steaming and expanding the cake. See page 26 for more information.

The sugar is added to the egg whites gradually, 1 tablespoon (15 g) at a time, right after a foam starts to form. When it looks like a bubble bath, that's a sign that the proteins have started to trap air. Once we add the sugar, we need to stay close and make sure we stop the whipping once the meringue reaches soft-medium peaks.

The way to know it's done is by dipping the whisk in the meringue, then turning it over right side up, so the meringue is facing the ceiling. If the meringue creates a soft ribbon that rolls downward but still holds its shape, it's ready. If the meringue doesn't hold any shape and drips down the whisk, it's too soft and needs to be whisked for a while longer. If it holds a firm pointy peak upward, it's too firm and you might need to start over (see page 129 for images).

Once the meringue is ready, we gently fold in the sifted flour mixture. We fold in the flour in three additions; this is so the weight of the flour mixture doesn't deflate the meringue.

My Strawberry Angel Food Cake recipe has the addition of freeze-dried strawberry powder, and because there's a small amount of pectin in the powder, it might not rise as high as it normally would. Despite that, the cake is still tall, light and tender with a beautiful pink hue and a refreshing, sweet strawberry flavor.

STRAWBERRY ANGEL FOOD CAKE

This recipe is a great example of the angel food cake ratio and mixing method.

YIELD: One 9 x 4–inch (23 x 10–cm) cake

1 cup (120 g) cake flour

2 tbsp (16 g) freeze-dried strawberry powder

1¾ cups (350 g) granulated sugar, divided

12 large egg whites

½ tsp cream of tartar

2 tsp (10 ml) strawberry extract

TOPPING

1 cup (240 ml) heavy cream

2 tbsp (30 g) granulated sugar

1 cup (225 g) fresh strawberries, cut in half

¼ cup pistachios, shelled and minced

Preheat the oven to 325°F (160°C) and have a 9 x 4–inch (23 x 10–cm) angel food pan ready. Don't grease the pan.

In a large bowl, sift together the flour and strawberry powder. Repeat three times, then stir in ¾ cup (150 g) of sugar.

In the bowl of a stand mixer fitted with the whisk attachment, place the egg whites and cream of tartar. Have the remaining 1 cup (200 g) of sugar ready to use. Whisk on low speed, gradually increasing the mixer speed to medium-high. Once a foamy-looking meringue forms, sprinkle in the remaining sugar 1 tablespoon (15 g) at a time, waiting 10 seconds before adding the next. Whisk the eggs to a medium peak, then stop the mixer.

Gently fold in the strawberry extract, then fold in the flour-sugar mixture in three additions.

Pour the batter into the pan and bake on the middle rack for 40 to 45 minutes. The cake is ready when a toothpick inserted into the center of the cake comes out clean and the top of the cake is brown and dry.

Remove the cake from the oven, then gently invert it and let it cool for 2 hours upside down. If you notice that the tube part of the cake is sliding down after you invert the cake, turn it up again and bake it for an additional 5 minutes.

To make the topping, in a large bowl place the heavy cream and sugar, then mix using the whisk attachment on low, gradually increasing speed to high. Mix until the cream has thickened.

Once the cake has cooled completely, run a knife around the sides of the pan, then remove the cake, on the bottom of the pan, from the pan. Now, run the knife along the bottom of the cake and around the tube of the cake and gently lift it and place it on a serving plate.

Top the cake with whipped cream, decorate with fresh strawberries and sprinkle with pistachios.

The cake can be stored covered at room temperature for up to 3 days.

Always Light Meringue

Meringue is used for many reasons in the baking world. It can help leaven our baked goods like we saw in the angel food cake (page 127), it can provide volume to our recipe like when we make Italian meringue buttercream (page 129) and sometimes it's made to enjoy as is like in the following recipe for delicious and addictive Caramel-Filled Meringue Clouds (page 131).

They're the most delicious and unique treat. A light and thick meringue filled with caramel and sprinkled with salt flakes is baked until the top is dry and crispy but the center is fluffy and soft. The combinations of crispy and soft and sweet and salty make this recipe a one-of-a-kind flavorful experience.

Meringue Ratio:
Egg Whites 100%; Sugar 0–200%

Mixing Method

Meringue is a stabilized foam. When we whip egg whites, the protein chains in the egg whites unfold, denature and make their way toward each other to bond together (see page 26 for more information).

During that process, the air we're whipping into the egg whites is trapped in between the bonds of the unfolded proteins chains, creating a stabilized, thick, light and opaque foam.

The amount of time and the amount of sugar we incorporate into the egg whites will determine the strength and stability of the meringue. The longer we whip, the more air we incorporate—and the stronger the bonds of the proteins are.

If we whip for too long, the proteins might bond too tightly and squeeze the water out and break our foam. To prevent that from happening, we add cream of tartar (page 64) and sugar.

Sugar is an important foam stabilizer; it absorbs the liquids that surround the air bubbles and the proteins, giving the proteins more space to trap more air while increasing its stability—keeping the foam from breaking. The amount of sugar can be varied, from no sugar at all to up to double the amount of the egg whites. The more sugar we add, the more stabilized our foam will be.

There are four types of meringues: plain meringue, French meringue, Italian meringue and Swiss meringue.

Plain meringue: Whipped egg whites without the addition of sugar; this meringue isn't very stable.

French meringue: Whip the egg whites until a light foam forms, then gradually add the sugar and whip until stabilized and thick. This meringue isn't as stabilized as the following two and can break more easily and faster, which is why paying attention to the amount of sugar and whipping time is very important.

Soft Meringue

Medium Peak

Stiff Peak

Swiss meringue: Whip the eggs and sugar over a double boiler until the sugar has dissolved, then remove from heat and whip until stabilized and thick. Since we dissolve the sugar with the egg whites, the sugar had a chance to absorb the water from the egg whites and create a strong bond with the water, giving the proteins in the egg whites a chance to trap more air. That makes this meringue a very stable one (see page 58 for more information).

Italian meringue: Cook sugar with water until sugar reaches 242°F (116°C), then drizzle the sugar into the egg whites while whipping until a thick and stabilized foam forms. Since we dissolve the sugar, the sugar is now an inverted sugar (aka a syrup). As a syrup and its two molecules, the fructose and glucose, have been separated. Fructose tends to caramelize faster, so Italian meringue, when baked, tends to have a darker, lightly caramelized color to it.

As we whip, it's easy to notice the changes in the stability of the meringue. The more we whip, the thicker and less transparent the foam is. Different meringues require the recipe to be in a different state of stability. A soft peak is when the meringue is white and opaque, but it's very soft and can be drizzled down. A medium peak is when the meringue is thick and stabilized but still is elastic enough to create a ribbon with a spoon. And, lastly, a stiff peak is when the meringue is very stiff—it will hold its shape even if we turn the bowl upside down.

Now that you're knowledgeable, test your skills by making these Caramel-Filled Meringue Clouds!

CARAMEL–FILLED MERINGUE CLOUDS

This recipe is a great example of the meringue ratio and mixing method.

YIELD: 12 meringue cookies

CARAMEL

½ cup (100 g) granulated sugar

⅛ tsp cream of tartar

2 tbsp (30 ml) water

¼ cup (60 ml) heavy cream

3 tbsp (42 g) unsalted butter, softened

MERINGUE

4 large egg whites

½ tsp cream of tartar

½ cup (100 g) granulated sugar

1 cup (120 g) powdered sugar

2 tbsp salt flakes

To make the caramel, in a wide skillet, mix the granulated sugar and cream of tartar, then add the water. Swirl the pan to make sure all the sugar is coated with water.

Cook the mixture on medium heat and don't stir it. If you notice some sugar crystallization on the sides of the pan, dip a small pastry brush in water and brush the sides of the pan.

Allow the sugar to cook until it turns a light golden color, 5 to 7 minutes. You'll notice that the first bubbles appear from the sides toward the center of the pan. Soon after, the sides will start to brown. If one section gets darker than the rest, change the position of the pan but do not stir the mixture.

Once the sugar has turned golden brown, turn off the heat and carefully add the cream while stirring. Then, add the butter and stir until it melts. Pour the caramel into a glass container and allow it to cool for a minimum of 3 hours before filling the meringue.

To make the meringue, preheat the oven to 215°F (100°C). Line a 13 x 18–inch (33 x 45–cm) rimmed cookie pan with parchment paper. Set aside.

(continued)

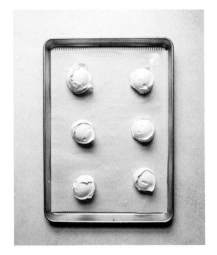  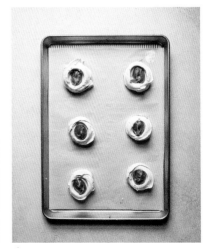

CARAMEL-FILLED MERINGUE CLOUDS (cont.)

In the bowl of a stand mixer fitted with the whisk attachment, place the egg whites and cream of tartar and beat on medium speed until frothy, about 1 minute.

Add the granulated sugar in four stages, waiting 20 seconds between each addition, then add the powdered sugar and beat until a stiff, shiny meringue forms. This should take 7 to 12 minutes depending on the strength of the mixer.

Halfway through the mixing process, when the meringue reaches a medium peak, stop the mixer and check its consistency between your thumb and pointer finger. If you feel not all of the sugar has dissolved, add up to 2 to 4 teaspoons (10 to 20 ml) of water 1 teaspoon at a time, mix for 10 seconds, then test it again before adding more water.

Using a large cookie spoon (holds 3 tablespoons [45 g]), spoon six scoops on the prepared pan, leaving 2 inches (5 cm) of space between each mound. Using a small spoon dipped with water, gently make a dent in the meringues, fill each dent with 1 teaspoon of cooled caramel, then top each with an additional scoop of meringue. Use your finger or a spoon to seal the gaps.

Sprinkle each cloud with a pinch of salt flakes and bake on the middle rack for 1 hour and 45 minutes. The meringues are ready when the tops are dry and they can be easily lifted from the pan without sticking to the parchment paper.

Store the meringues in a sealed container at room temperature for up to 3 days.

NOTES

The cookies sometimes crack and the caramel drizzles out. If you don't want that to happen, replace the powdered sugar with ¼ cup (50 g) of granulated sugar in the meringue ingredients.

Powdered sugar has cornstarch in it. The cornstarch molecules soak up some of the liquid and as the temperature rises during baking, they swell and "break" the meringue, causing the cookies to break.

The longer you bake the meringue, the firmer the cookies will be. If you prefer a crispy cookie, use only granulated sugar and increase the baking time to 2½ to 3 hours.

The cornstarch in the powdered sugar will provide the cookies a soft texture while the granulated sugar will eventually crystalize into a firm brittle texture.

Moist Quick Breads and Muffins You'll Master

Quick breads and muffins are easy and fast to make and are the best-known secret for a comforting breakfast or a fast snack. They rely on chemical leavening such as baking soda and baking powder. They tend to be dense and moist, and many times they lose their freshness within one day.

Quick Bread and Muffin Ratio:
Flour 100%; Eggs 50%; Fat 50%; Liquid 100%

Mixing Method

Well, when it comes to baking, it doesn't get easier than quick breads and muffins. Even the mixing method, named the one-stage method, implies how easy it is. All you have to do is sift the dry ingredients, then mix in the liquid, fat, eggs and other ingredients just until the flour has been incorporated.

The large amount of liquid in the batter will encourage a strong gluten bond, so to avoid a chewy and tough texture, the mixing process should be fast and minimal, just until the flour has been fully incorporated. If the batter isn't smooth and there are a few lumps, it's okay and they will dissolve during baking.

But having such a large amount of liquid in a recipe is a great thing. It's actually what makes muffins and quick breads so tender and delicious, and it gives us unlimited ways to flavor and elevate our recipes, like in the Reese's® Peanut Butter Quick Bread recipe (page 134).

To better infuse the peanuts' flavor, the milk is boiled with some roasted peanuts, then cooled to room temperature. As the milk's temperature rises, the peanuts' oil releases their flavors and rises to the surface, so by the time the milk has completely cooled, the milk tastes like peanuts.

The next step is to mix the ingredients using the one-stage method. The flour, baking powder, baking soda, cocoa powder, sugar and peanut butter chips are sifted and mixed together, then the milk, eggs and oil are poured over and mixed in to incorporate.

Using light brown sugar versus granulated sugar and vegetable oil versus melted butter is important, these ingredients provide even more moisture to the bread and prolong its shelf life by one to two days.

This Reese's® Peanut Butter Quick Bread is not only easy and fast to make, but it's also moist, soft, tender and full of nostalgic peanut butter and chocolate flavors.

REESE'S®
PEANUT BUTTER
QUICK BREAD

This recipe is a great example of the quick breads ratio and mixing method.

YIELD: Two 8-inch (20-cm) loaves

PEANUT MILK

1¼ cups (300 ml) whole milk

½ cup (73 g) roasted peanuts

BREAD

2 cups (250 g) all-purpose flour

½ cup (44 g) cocoa powder

1 cup (220 g) light brown sugar

1 tsp baking powder

¼ tsp baking soda

1 cup (168 g) Reese's® peanut butter chips

1 cup (240 ml) peanut milk, room temperature

2 large eggs, room temperature

½ cup (120 ml) vegetable oil

8–10 mini Reese's® peanut butter cups (optional)

NOTES

Make sure all of the ingredients are at room temperature.

You can skip making the peanut milk and use regular milk instead.

This recipe can be baked as muffins and will yield 12 regular-sized muffins, but adjust baking time to 18 to 22 minutes.

To make the peanut milk, in a medium saucepan, pour in the milk and add the peanuts. Bring the mixture to a boil, then immediately remove it from heat and let it cool to room temperature. Run the milk through a sieve; you should have 1 cup (240 ml) of milk. Discard the peanuts.

To make the bread, preheat the oven to 350°F (175°C) and grease two 8-inch (20-cm) loaf pans. Set aside.

In a large bowl, sift together the flour, cocoa powder, brown sugar, baking powder and baking soda. Add the peanut butter chips, then use a fork to incorporate the ingredients.

In a separate large bowl, pour the peanut milk, eggs and oil and mix to combine. Pour the milk mixture on top of the flour mixture. Mix using a hand whisk just until the ingredients have been incorporated and you no longer see dry flour. Fold in the Reese's mini cups, if using, then divide the batter between the two prepared pans.

Bake for 40 to 45 minutes on the middle rack, turning the pans halfway through. The loaves are ready when the tops appear puffed and dry and a toothpick inserted into the center of the loaves comes out dry or with few moist crumbs.

Remove the loaves from the oven and allow them to cool for 10 to 15 minutes before slicing.

The bread is best when eaten the same day and can be stored covered at room temperature for up to 2 days.

No-Fail Flaky Scones and Biscuits

Biscuits, scones and piecrusts all have different ratios, different textures and they all taste different. But interestingly enough, they all share the same mixing method. The change in ingredients and ratios is what gives each pastry its unique texture, flavor and appearance.

The first and, by far, the most important step in making pastries is making sure the ingredients are as cold as possible. That means measuring the butter, flour and liquid ahead of time and placing them back in the refrigerator or freezer if possible.

Why? Let's check out the science!

Well, when we bite into a scone or a slice of pie, the texture should be flaky, tender and crumbly. The way to achieve that is by minimizing the development of gluten; however, gluten is very important in providing structure and bringing the ingredients together. It's a delicate balancing act to make sure that enough gluten chains form to give the pastry structure, but not too many or too strong, which would result in tough, dry pastries. We encountered this issue when we made Butternut Squash–Caramelized Onion Galette (page 34) and we used starch as a way to balance this act.

Another great way to control and monitor the development of gluten—which is true in all pastry-making processes—is by making sure that each ingredient is doing only what it's supposed to do.

Let's take, for example, fat or, in this recipe, butter. We talked about the importance of fat and butter in the baking world, and now we know that the butter's job is to provide flavor, tenderness and flakiness. In this case, scones are made by coating the flour granules with butter, so when we add the liquid, the fat-coated flour will not absorb as much water as it would otherwise.

Since butter is more than 10 percent water, if added warm, the butter will melt, releasing the water and, as a result, the flour will absorb the water before it's coated with fat and start the development of gluten.

The butter also provides flakiness to our pastries. As the water in the butter melts, it evaporates into steam, "lifting" the flour and creating air pockets, which we see as those flaky layers we love so much.

This is why the remaining ingredients are also incorporated into the doughs as cold as possible, to prevent them from melting the fat and contributing to the unwanted development of gluten.

Scones and Biscuits

The fun and best part about this ratio and mixing method is that we can use it to make sweet and tender scones, as well as savory and flaky biscuits.

And it's not hard to bake these delicious tender and flavorful scones. It's all in the technique!

Scone and Biscuit Ratio:
Flour 100%; Fat 30–50%; Liquid 70%

Mixing Method

The very first steps in making scones or biscuits are to measure and cool the ingredients. In the Apricot–White Chocolate Scones recipe (page 139), the instructions call to use a vegetable grater to grate the butter. This is so we minimize the time cutting the butter into the flour mixture and to prevent the butter from melting as we do so.

Grating the butter using a cheese grater will reduce the time it takes to incorporate the butter into the flour.

Cut the butter into the flour until it resembles a lightly damp sand with no dry flour.

Partly hydrated dough with some dry flour indicates more liquid should be added.

A properly hydrated dough comes together when pressed.

When the flour mixture resembles damp, wet sand, it's an indication that the butter is coating the flour properly. At this point, we can add our add-ins—the apricots and white chocolate chips—followed by the cold liquid.

When you add extra ingredients like these, they might cause the scones to overspread and lose their shape. To stop this from happening, all you have to do is add an egg to help bind the scone together. (Read more about eggs binding baked goods on page 26.)

Like we mentioned in the introduction to scones and biscuits, we should only add enough water to bring the dough together and create the smallest gluten development. In the Apricot–White Chocolate Scones recipe, even though it calls for more than 1 cup (240 ml) of liquid, the instructions call to initially drizzle only two-thirds of the liquid.

This is because different types of flour absorb water differently. Factors such as your climate and kitchen temperature may impact the moisture in the dough; humid climates tend to absorb more moisture into the batter than dry climates.

So, we start by adding only two-thirds of the liquids and mixing them in with a wooden spoon—not kneading, only mixing. Turning the flour with the spoon helps it absorb the liquid without developing the gluten. The act of kneading the dough will encourage a strong gluten bond that might cause tough scones.

If the liquid has been fully absorbed but there's still some dry flour, then we'll add more liquid, 1 tablespoon (15 ml) at a time. But, if the flour has been fully absorbed, then it's time to divide and cut the scones.

Use the leftover liquid to brush the scones before baking. It will encourage the browning of the scones and provide a soft, tender texture.

We take an extra step and place the unbaked scones in the refrigerator or freezer while the oven is preheating. The low temperature will help to set the butter and maintain the shape of the scones during baking.

These Apricot–White Chocolate Scones are firm yet tender and flaky. The addition of spices enhances the apricots' flavor, while the white chocolate complements the fruit's tanginess.

APRICOT–WHITE CHOCOLATE SCONES

This recipe is a great example of the scones ratio and mixing method.

YIELD: 8 medium-sized scones

---

10 tbsp (150 g) unsalted butter, cold

1 large egg, cold

1 cup (240 ml) half-and-half, cold, plus more as needed for brushing

3 cups (375 g) all-purpose flour

2 tsp (9 g) baking powder

1 tsp ground cinnamon

½ tsp ground ginger

¼ tsp ground cardamom

¼ tsp ground cloves

¼ cup (50 g) granulated sugar

½ cup (80 g) chopped dried apricots

1 cup (168 g) white chocolate chips

Use a cheese or vegetable grater to grate the butter, then place it back in the refrigerator to cool while you get the rest of the ingredients ready.

In a large measuring cup, beat the egg, then pour it over the half-and-half and mix to blend. Place the mixture in the refrigerator. Line a 13 x 18–inch (33 x 45–cm) large cookie pan with parchment paper and set aside.

In a large bowl, sift the flour, baking powder, cinnamon, ginger, cardamom and cloves. Add the sugar, then use a fork to fully incorporate the ingredients. Add the cold butter into the flour mixture and use the tip of your fingers or a fork to cut the butter into the flour until it resembles wet sand. This should take 2 to 3 minutes and the butter should remain cold and should not stick to your hands. If your fingers get sticky with soft butter, place the bowl back in the refrigerator (or freezer) to cool for 10 to 15 minutes, or until the butter sets again.

Sprinkle the apricots and white chocolate chips into a large bowl and toss to incorporate.

Drizzle ⅔ cup (160 ml) of the half-and-half mixture into the flour mixture, and with a fork or a rubber spatula, incorporate the liquids into the flour and butter mixture until all of the flour has been hydrated. If needed, add some of the remaining liquid 1 tablespoon (15 ml) at a time.

Place the dough onto a clean work surface and press it together with your hands, then fold it over itself.

Divide the dough into two equal parts and shape each part into a 3 x 6–inch (8 x 15–cm) or a 4 x 8–inch (10 x 20–cm) rectangle for thinner scones. Cut each rectangle at the center so you'll have two squares, then cut each square into two triangles and place each triangle on the prepared pan. Lightly brush the scones with the remaining liquid. If you don't have any, use heavy cream, then place the pan in the refrigerator.

Preheat oven to 350°F (175°C). On the middle rack, bake for 20 to 22 minutes, or until the edges and bottoms of the scones start to brown and the tops look dry. Remove the scones from the oven and let them cool for 10 to 15 minutes before serving.

The scones are best eaten the same day and can be stored in an airtight container at room temperature for up to 2 days.

NOTE

I like to add the egg whenever I have add-ins to the scones, since the egg helps keep the shape of the scones and allows me to shape the scones a bit thicker. You can skip the egg, but make sure to shape the scones thinner.

The Perfect Piecrust

If you follow the formula below, you'll end up with the perfect piecrust: a tender, melt-in-your-mouth crust, full of beautiful air pockets and a delicious buttery flavor.

Piecrust Ratio: Flour 100%; Fat 66%; Liquid 33%

Mixing Method

Many bakers scratch their heads when, instead of a tender and flaky piecrust, they end up with a tough dough with no layers or sometimes even a soggy piecrust.

Let's troubleshoot and figure out what causes those problems and how we can fix them.

The crust is tough.

The only way to know whether our crust is tender or tough is by tasting it. A tough crust, while it can keep its flakiness, is too firm when we bite it, and it doesn't easily break as we chew it. This occurs when we don't fully incorporate the butter into the flour mixture and some of the flour granules remain uncoated with butter. So when adding the liquid to the dough, the uncoated flour granules absorb the liquid and creates a tight gluten bond that bakes into a tough texture.

To avoid that from happening, make sure you cut the butter into the flour, until the flour resembles lightly damp sand. You can use a food processor, a stand mixer, a pastry cutter or even a fork.

The crust is tender but not flaky.

When the piecrust is tender but doesn't have any flaky layers, it means that the butter has been incorporated well but there were not enough "chunks" of butter pieces to "lift" the dough during the baking process as the butter was melting.

The best way to ensure the crust is both tender and flaky is by dividing the butter into two parts, two-thirds of the butter being cut into small pieces. Those small pieces will coat the flour and make sure the crust will bake into a tender texture. The remaining one-third of the butter amount should be cut into larger pieces that will remain large as we incorporate the liquid, so then later when the dough is baking, there are enough large pieces of butter that have the ability to puff the dough and create beautiful flaky layers.

Another way to create a flaky crust is by using the fraisage method. *Fraisage* is a fancy French term that means "smearing." We smear the dough with the heel of our hand, and by doing that, the butter in the dough is changing its shape from tiny chunks to flat ones. So when we bake, those flat butter pieces will melt and evaporate easily while still creating air pockets.

You can do one technique or the other, but I highly recommend doing both, like in the following Tender and Flaky Piecrust recipe (page 142).

It has a soggy bottom.

Oh oh . . . sorry to hear that. If your pie has a soggy bottom, it means that the ingredients were not cold enough and melted the butter or you added too much water to the dough. When that happens, instead of making piecrust, you basically make cookie dough that tends to soak up all the liquids coming from the pie filling.

Make sure your ingredients are as cold as they can possibly be and that you add the smallest amount of liquid to the dough.

The dough is shrinking.

Let's start with the fact that every piecrust dough shrinks. It's not a bad thing, that's why we have pie weights. Piecrust shrinks because the gluten bond of the dough is very weak, and once the butter melts, it breaks that bond even further. As a result, the gluten chains shrink back almost to their original size. In addition, the liquid in the starches evaporates, shrinking the starches' size.

The problem is when the dough shrinks too much, even when we use piecrust weights, and there are a few reasons it might happen. The first one is when we don't coat the flour with butter well enough, and as the butter melts, it reaches those areas of flour and disturbs the bond.

Another reason is when we don't give enough resting time to the dough before rolling it. The resting time is very important—it allows the starches in the flour to absorb the water and swell. If we skip this part, then the starches are not hydrated enough. They're not swollen enough to maintain their size during baking, and as we bake, they lose most of the liquid and shrink.

My Tender and Flaky Piecrust recipe includes all the steps that will prevent the above issues from happening, ensuring that you'll end up with a delicious, tender and flaky crust.

In the recipe, the very first step calls to measure, cut and refrigerate the ingredients at least 30 minutes before we mix the dough. Cold ingredients help us control the formation of strong gluten chains, as we learned in the pastry section introduction (page 136).

The recipe can be made using a bowl and a pastry cutter or a fork—or in a stand mixer.

To make sure the crust is both tender and flaky, we divide the butter into two parts. Then, cut one part of the butter into ¼-inch (6-mm) pieces and the second part into ½-inch (1.3-cm) pieces. The smaller pieces will coat the flour and provide a tender texture, while the larger pieces will ensure there is enough butter to create layers.

Also, the fraisage method is incorporated to create even more flaky layers.

And lastly, the dough is wrapped in a plastic bag and refrigerated for a minimum of two hours to make sure the butter is firming up and the starches found in the flour are hydrating.

The type of flour we use when we bake piecrust makes a big difference. The next recipe calls for bleached all-purpose flour that tends to have a lower percentage of gluten. You can also use pastry flour and follow the recipe as is, or unbleached all-purpose flour with the addition of potato starch (see the Butternut Squash–Caramelized Onion Galette recipe on page 34).

TENDER AND FLAKY PIECRUST

This recipe is a great example of the piecrust ratio and mixing method.

YIELD: One 9-inch (23-cm) pie or one 8-inch (20-cm) galette

1¼ cups (156 g) bleached all-purpose flour

⅛ tsp baking powder

¼ tsp salt

7 tbsp (98 g) unsalted butter, cold

1 tbsp (15 ml) apple cider vinegar

3–4 tbsp (45–60 ml) ice water

To prepare the ingredients, in a plastic bag, measure the flour, baking powder and salt. Stir to blend, then place the mixture in the freezer for a minimum of 30 minutes.

Divide the butter into two parts: 5 tablespoons (70 g) and 2 tablespoons (28 g). Cut the larger portion into ¼-inch (6-mm) pieces and the smaller portion into ½-inch (1.3-cm) pieces. Wrap each part with plastic wrap, then place them in the refrigerator for a minimum of 30 minutes.

To make the dough, in a large bowl (or the bowl of a stand mixer), place the flour mixture and add the smaller butter pieces. Use your fingers to cover the butter with flour, then use a fork or a pastry cutter (if using a stand mixer, use the paddle attachment on medium-low speed) to cut the butter into the flour until the flour resembles slightly wet sand.

Add the larger butter pieces and cut them into the flour until they're the size of large peas.

Sprinkle the vinegar and 3 tablespoons (45 ml) of water, then toss the mixture using a rubber spatula or a rubber bench scraper to incorporate the water into the mixture. If you notice big clumps of dough, use the spatula to cut into it. This will help distribute the water to the remaining dry flour.

Grab a small piece of dough and bring it together with your hands. If it sticks together, then your dough is ready; if it crumbles, then add the remaining 1 tablespoon (15 ml) of ice water and toss again. Dump the mixture on a clean work surface and bring it together with your hands to form a small mound.

Using the heels of your hands, rub the dough, starting at the top of the mound and all the way down the dough and going about 2 inches (5 cm) into your work surface. Repeat this with the remaining dough, then press the dough together into a disc shape. Cover the dough with a plastic bag and refrigerate it for a minimum of 2 hours.

When ready to bake, remove the dough from the refrigerator and sprinkle your work surface with a very light dusting of flour. Roll the dough, turning it 90 degrees every two rolls to make sure it will not stick to the surface. If needed, sprinkle with some more flour.

This dough can be used as a base for pies, galettes, mini pies or cut using a cookie cutter and eaten as a delicious snack.

For pies and galettes, follow the instructions of the recipe when baking. To bake piecrust snacks, preheat the oven to 425°F (218°C). Brush the piecrust with egg wash and bake on the lower rack for 12 minutes, or until golden and puffed.

Make sure to place the rolled dough back in the refrigerator for a minimum of 30 minutes before baking.

Incredibly Easy to Personalize Cookies

Cookies come in a large variety of textures. They can be crispy and flat, chubby and chewy and even soft and tender. Once you understand the science we cover here, you can tailor and personalize a cookie recipe by adding or reducing ingredients and playing with the ratio. For a chewy cookie, choose melted butter and brown sugar; for a crispy and flat cookie, make sure you increase the amount of butter and add some baking soda to the recipe. Chapters 1 (page 10) and 2 (page 16) cover the science behind these different ingredients.

Cookie Ratio:
Flour 100%; Fat 66%; Sugar 33%

The cookie ratio—also known as the one, two, three ratio—is one of the most commonly used ratios, especially when baking shortbread cookies, like the ones on page 145.

Mixing Method

There are as many different mixing methods for cookies as there are cookies, and no one is better than the other. Chocolate chip cookie recipes often instruct you to aerate the butter with the sugar, while madeleines are made using the aeration of the eggs with the sugar.

The Flower Blossom Shortbread Cookies (page 145) are crumbly, soft and buttery cookies. They're not only addictively delicious, but they're also made using a unique mixing method you can adapt to your baking repertoire. This recipe is a great example of how this cookie ratio can be personalized by the mixing method into the most flavorful cookies.

The recipe is made using a food processor, a great way to incorporate the ingredients without overworking the gluten and to make sure the cookies are tender and crumbly. It gets its flavor from the small amount of ground toasted almonds and the fat coming from the butter and egg yolk.

Notice that the recipe calls for a "pliable" butter (this typically happens at temperatures of 63 to 65°F [17 to 18°C]). A pliable butter is when the butter isn't as firm as it is when first we take it out of the refrigerator and also not as soft as when it reaches room temperature (it can be pressed easily but still keep a firm structure.). The reason we use a pliable butter is because it will easily coat the flour granules with fat and, at the same time, it will not release any of its water that might encourage the formation of gluten.

When the dough comes together, since it's very soft and might break as we transfer it to the pan, we roll it between two large pieces of parchment paper and let it rest for about 30 minutes, until the butter has firmed and the cookies can be easily cut and transferred to the cookie pan.

During the baking process, the color and type of pan we use to bake the cookies is very important.

Dark-colored cookie pans will absorb and provide more heat from the oven to the cookies, resulting in darker edges and bottoms. If needed, when using dark-colored pans, consider lowering the oven temperature or the baking time. Light-color cookie pans will reflect the heat back to the oven space and, as a result, the cookies will absorb less heat, resulting in lighter edges and bottoms.

Cookies that are baked in pans with no rims will absorb more heat from the oven and will bake faster than they would if baked in a rimmed cookie pan.

For the next recipe, I recommend using a light-colored rimmed cookie pan. If using a dark-colored pan, reduce the baking time by 2 minutes.

You can fill the cookies with Nutella®, your favorite jam or nothing at all, but I highly recommend you use the accompanying strawberry jam. The jam provides a sweet strawberry flavor and a moist and tender texture.

FLOWER BLOSSOM SHORTBREAD COOKIES

This recipe is a great example of the cookie ratio and mixing method.

YIELD: Twelve 2-inch (5-cm) double cookies

JAM

2½ cups (415 g) fresh strawberries (cut into ¼-inch [6-mm] pieces)

¾ cup (150 g) granulated sugar

1 tbsp (15 ml) fresh-squeezed lemon juice

½ tsp salt

1½ tsp (1 g) gelatin

1 tbsp (15 ml) water

COOKIES

⅓ cup (36 g) toasted slivered almonds

1¼ cups (156 g) all-purpose flour

¼ cup (50 g) granulated sugar

½ cup (114 g) unsalted butter, pliable

1 large egg yolk

¼ cup (30 g) powdered sugar to dust the cookies

(continued)

FLOWER BLOSSOM SHORTBREAD COOKIES (cont.)

To make the jam, in a medium pan, place the strawberries, sugar, lemon juice and salt and bring to a boil while stirring occasionally. Once boiling, reduce the heat to low and allow it to cook for 25 to 30 minutes, until the strawberries have softened and the liquid has thickened.

In a small bowl, place the gelatin and water and stir. Let the mixture sit for 3 minutes, until the gelatin has absorbed the water. Warm the bowl in the microwave for 3 to 4 seconds, then add it to the strawberry mixture. Cook for an additional 5 minutes. Remove it from heat and pour the jam into a medium glass container or a large mason jar.

As the jam cools, it will thicken. It's best stored in the refrigerator for up to 1 month.

To make the cookies, in a food processor, place the almonds and pulse eight times, until the almonds resemble a coarse meal (each pulse should be about 2 seconds).

Add the flour and granulated sugar and pulse five more times. Cut the butter into 1-inch (2.5-cm) pieces and add it to the flour mixture, then pulse five more times. Add the egg yolk and pulse five to seven times, just until the dough comes together.

Place the dough between two 13 x 18–inch (33 x 45–cm) large pieces of parchment paper. If needed, bring the dough together with your hands. Use a rolling pin to roll the dough to ¼-inch (6-mm) thick, then place it in the refrigerator to cool for about 30 minutes. Avoid cooling the dough for more than 2 hours. A long cooling time might dry the top layer of the dough and, as the cookies bake, the tops of the cookies might crack or have an unpleasant appearance.

When the cookies are ready to bake, preheat the oven to 335°F (168°C) and line a 13 x 18–inch (33 x 45–cm) cookie pan with parchment paper.

Remove the dough from the refrigerator and peel off the parchment paper. Use a 2-inch (5-cm) flower-shaped cookie cutter to cut the dough. Use a 1-inch (2.5-cm) round cookie cutter to cut a circle in the center of half of the cookies. Remove the centers. Reroll the leftover dough and refrigerate it, if needed, then cut the shapes again.

Bake for 12 to 14 minutes on the middle rack, or until the bottom edges of the cookies start to brown and the tops are dry to the touch. Remove from the oven and allow to cool in the pan for 10 minutes before transferring to a cookie rack.

Once the cookies have completely cooled, fill the center of an uncut cookie with ½ teaspoon of strawberry jam, then place a cut cookie on top and gently press. Dust with powdered sugar.

The cookies are best stored in an airtight container at room temperature unfilled for up to 10 days and filled for up to 5 days.

NOTE

Once the cookies are filled, the jam will soften the cookies.

Ganache for Every Occasion

I can't think of a better example of how science can elevate our baking skills than what it brings to making ganache. Ganache is a simple mixture of chopped chocolate and scalded heavy cream. It's one of the most familiar uses of chocolate and it's great for filling truffles, pastries and cakes, as well as for topping and decorating cakes and cupcakes.

The ganache firmness and structure can be altered to better fit our needs. It can be soft, firm or very firm.

Soft ganache is liquid and it's great for drizzling on ice cream or cakes—or even dipping cookies. It's made using double the amount of heavy cream in comparison to chocolate. Sometimes a small amount of corn syrup (1 tablespoon [15 ml] for 1 cup [206 g] of chocolate), vegetable oil or honey is added to provide an attractive glossy finish.

Firm ganache, unlike its name, is actually soft, but it's firm enough to hold its shape and not drip down. It's good for filling cakes, truffles or pastries and topping cupcakes. Firm ganache is made with equal parts heavy cream and chocolate. Other ingredients—such as butter, egg yolks or sugar—might be added for richness. You can substitute part of the heavy cream with juice or a smooth fruit puree for flavor.

Very firm ganache holds it shape very well and is best used to coat cakes that later might be covered with fondant.

Soft Ganache Ratio:
Chocolate 100%; Heavy Cream 200%

Firm Ganache Ratio:
Chocolate 100%; Heavy Cream 100%

Very Firm Ganache Ratio:
Chocolate 200%; Heavy Cream 100%

Different types of chocolate have different percentages of chocolate liquor, milk solids and sugar, and each type requires different amounts of heavy cream and chocolate to achieve the different types of ganache.

Chocolate liquor forms when the cocoa nibs are processed through large rollers, producing a warm liquid chocolate, which hardens into firm blocks when cooled. Those blocks are known as unsweetened chocolate, and the liquor refers to the chocolate when in a liquid warm phase (there's no alcohol in it).

Different amounts of milk solids and sugar are added to the chocolate liquor to make different types of chocolate, such as semisweet and milk chocolate. And the higher the percentage of chocolate liquor, the more intense the chocolate flavor is—including its bitterness.

On the next page is a table with ratios for different types of chocolate. Know that since each brand is different and doesn't always provide the same cocoa (chocolate liquor) percentage, you might have to make some small changes as you go by adding more chocolate or more cream.

Chocolate Type	Soft Ganache	Firm Ganache	Very Firm Ganache
Semisweet (56–65% cocoa)	Chocolate 100%; Heavy cream 150–200%	Chocolate 100%; Heavy cream 100%	Chocolate 200%; Heavy cream 100%
Milk chocolate (34–45% cocoa)	Chocolate 100%; Heavy cream 125–150%	Chocolate 200%; Heavy cream 100%	Chocolate 300%; Heavy cream 100%
White chocolate (30–35% cocoa butter only)	Chocolate 100%; Heavy cream 100%	Chocolate 250–300%; Heavy cream 100%	Chocolate 400%; Heavy cream 100%

Mixing Method

The mixing method of ganache is as simple as its ingredients. Scalded milk is poured over the chopped chocolate, allowing it three to four minutes to melt the chocolate. Then, it's gently mixed until a smooth ganache forms.

Make sure not to allow the heavy cream to boil. If boiled, the high temperature might break the crystal bond (see page 103 for more information) of the chocolate and the fat will separate from the mixture.

The Chocolate Ganache recipe (page 150) is for a firm ganache. It's perfect for filling cakes, cupcakes or pastries, as well as frosting cakes and cupcakes. The addition of light brown sugar adds flavor and moistens the ganache and, as a result, the ganache is smooth—soft yet firm enough to hold its shape when frosted. The honey adds the beautiful and attractive glossy look.

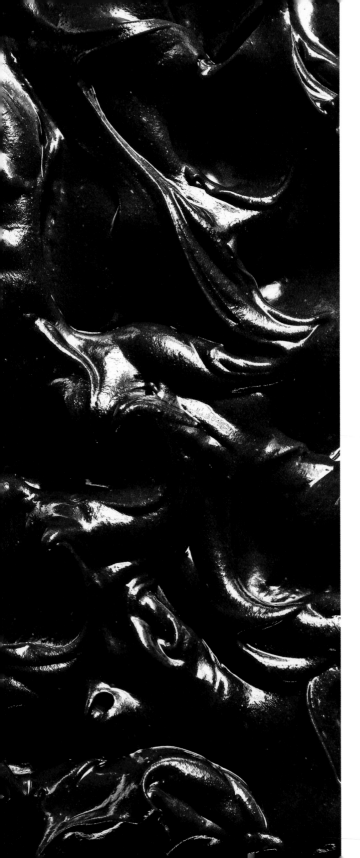

CHOCOLATE GANACHE

This recipe is a great example of the ganache ratio and mixing method.

YIELD: 1½ cups (396 g) ganache

1 cup (240 ml) heavy cream

¼ cup (55 g) light brown sugar

½ tsp salt

1¼ cups (220 g) chopped semisweet or dark chocolate

2 tsp (10 ml) honey

In a medium saucepan, pour the cream, then add the brown sugar and salt. Cook over medium heat until the sugar has dissolved and the mixture starts to simmer.

Pour the milk mixture over the chopped chocolate and let sit for 4 minutes.

Use a wooden spoon or a hand whisk to gently stir the chocolate with the cream until it's smooth and glossy. Then, mix in the honey and allow it to cool to room temperature so it's firm.

The ganache is ready to be used once it's at room temperature. It can be stored at room temperature for up to 3 days.

Consistently Creamy Custard

For many years, I stayed away from baking any custardy dessert because it seemed so complicated and scary. But the truth is that the science behind it is fairly simple, and it opens countless doors for unlimited sophisticated and impressive recipes.

Custard Ratio:
Eggs 100%; Liquid 200%

Custard, whether freestanding or not, is a mixture of cream or milk and eggs, and sometimes sugar or other flavorings are added. The mixture is then thickened during the cooking or baking process as a result of coagulation (page 26).

One egg can thicken ½ cup (120 ml) of liquids (cream or milk) into a stabilized freestanding custard like the Cheesy Salmon Quiche recipe (page 152). If we mix one egg or three egg yolks with 2 cups (480 ml) of cream or milk, it will thicken the liquid into an eggnog-like mixture. That's because the less the eggs are diluted with liquids and other ingredients, the closer the proteins are to each other and the easier it is for them to bond.

Freestanding custard must include whole eggs or egg whites in order for the custard to be sliced or removed from a dish. Since egg yolks contain fat, their proteins are less efficient in bonding and creating a firm coagulation network than the egg whites. That's also the reason why egg yolks coagulate at a higher temperature than egg whites and it explains why so often custard and cream recipes call for egg yolks only. In addition to its weaker coagulation, the fat provides a smooth texture and flavor.

Many times, starches such as cornstarch or flour are added to increase the temperature of egg coagulation by absorbing the liquid, swelling and getting in the eggs' way, stopping the eggs from coagulating too soon or too tight.

Even though different recipes call for different methods, there are some similarities to all custards, which we cover below.

Most freestanding recipes are mixed by beating the eggs with the liquids, then pouring them over the fruits, vegetables or into the dish. Fruits and vegetables will release their liquids into the dish, creating air pockets that surround them, so it would be a good idea to precook the fruits or vegetables if possible.

Some recipes call for cooking custard over the stove. If that's the case, it's very important to cook it over low heat (using a double boiler is a great option) and to resist the temptation of increasing the heat, even if it seems like nothing is actually happening. Turning up the heat is the difference between a soft and creamy custard and a crude one.

If a recipe calls to scald the liquid, then mix it with the eggs, always making sure to add the hot ingredients into the cold ones and not vice versa. When slowly adding the warm liquid to the eggs, the liquid is increasing the eggs' temperature to one that's lower than the setting temperature. When adding the eggs to the warm liquids, the eggs will immediately reach a setting temperature, causing them to set and curdle.

When baking custards, whether using a water bath or not, it's important to remove the custard from the oven or turn off the heat before the center has fully set and while it still jiggles. Then, allow it to fully set as it cools down.

(continued)

CONSISTENTLY CREAMY CUSTARD (cont.)

Let's take a closer look at the delicious Cheesy Salmon Quiche. A total of 1½ cups (360 ml) of liquid are thickened with three eggs; each egg is thickening ½ cup (120 ml) of liquid. This ratio of eggs to liquid is what helps the custard in the quiche to bind together the onions, dill and salmon—and it's why we're able to remove a slice individually.

Know that we can replace one egg with two egg yolks with no concern that the custard might not firm well enough. The heavy cream doesn't contain as much water as the milk due to its high concentration of fat.

The onions are sautéed and the fish is cooked before we bake the quiche. This is because the custard doesn't cook the ingredients, it only binds them together by coagulating and firming the liquids or, in this case, the onions, dill and fish.

You may notice that the quiche is baked at a fairly high temperature of 375°F (190°C), but there isn't concern of the custard over-baking and curdling since the par-baked crust provides another layer of protection. Also, we turn the oven off before the quiche has a chance to fully set.

It only takes one bite of this amazing quiche to taste a celebration of flavors and textures. Along with a crumbly and buttery crust, the sautéed onions and dill complement the salmon as they all come together into a cheesy and tender custard. It only takes one bite to want another one and another one.

What makes this bite possible, and what brings all of those mouthwatering flavors and textures together, is the custard.

CHEESY SALMON QUICHE

This recipe is a great example of the custard ratio and mixing method.

YIELD: One 9-inch (23-cm) quiche

CRUST

1½ cups (188 g) bleached all-purpose flour

⅛ tsp baking powder

¼ tsp salt

½ cup (114 g) unsalted butter, cold

1 tbsp (15 ml) apple cider vinegar

1 large egg yolk

4 tbsp (60 ml) milk

FILLING

¾ cup (180 ml) heavy cream

¾ cup (180 ml) whole milk

3 large eggs, lightly beaten

2 small shallots, chopped and sautéed

2 tbsp (7 g) chopped fresh dill

¾ cup (75 g) grated Parmesan cheese, divided

½ tsp salt

¼ tsp ground black pepper

1 cup (136 g) cooked salmon (cut into ½-inch [1.3-cm] pieces)

(continued)

CHEESY SALMON QUICHE (cont.)

To make the crust, in a plastic bag, measure the flour, baking powder and salt. Shake the bag to incorporate the ingredients, then place it in the freezer for a minimum of 30 minutes.

Cut the butter into ½-inch (1.3-cm) pieces, wrap them in a plastic bag and place them in the refrigerator for a minimum of 30 minutes.

In a food processor, place the flour mixture and process for 5 seconds. Add the butter and pulse for 2 seconds five times. The butter should be the size of large peas. Add the vinegar, egg yolk, and milk and pulse again for 2 seconds five times. The butter should now be the size of small peas and the mixture should resemble wet sand and shouldn't come together unless you press it with your fingers.

Dump the mixture on a clean work surface and bring it together into a small mound with your hands. Using the heel of your hands, smear the dough from the top toward the bottom, about 2 inches (5 cm) from the edge. Repeat with the remaining dough.

Bring the dough together with your hands into a disc shape—don't knead it—and wrap it in a plastic bag. Place it in the refrigerator and cool for a minimum of 2 hours or overnight.

When ready to bake the crust, lightly dust your work surface with flour and roll the dough into a 13-inch (33-cm) circle. Make sure to turn the dough 90 degrees as you roll to prevent it from sticking to the surface. Fold the dough in half, then fold it in half again so it looks like a triangle. Lift the dough and place the top of the triangle at the center of your pie dish, then unfold it. Gently press the dough into the sides of the pan, making sure there are no gaps between the pan and the dough. Place it back in the refrigerator to chill while the oven warms up.

Preheat the oven to 425°F (218°C) and place a cookie pan on the lower rack. Remove the pie dish from the refrigerator and prick the bottom and sides of the dough. Spray a large piece of parchment paper with oil spray, press it into the pie dough, then fill the dish with pie weights.

Bake for 15 minutes, then remove the piecrust from the oven. Allow it to cool for 10 minutes, then remove the pie weights and bake again for 5 minutes. Remove the piecrust from the oven and let it cool while you make the filling.

Reduce the oven temperature to 375°F (190°C). In a large bowl, mix the cream, milk and eggs. In another large bowl, place the shallots, dill, ½ cup (50 g) of Parmesan cheese, salt and pepper, then pour the egg mixture on top and stir to distribute the liquids. Pour the mixture into the par-baked pie dish, then sprinkle in the salmon pieces. Bake for 40 minutes on the middle rack. Thirty minutes into baking, sprinkle on the remaining ¼ cup (25 g) of the Parmesan cheese.

The quiche is ready when the edges are set but the center jiggles when you move the pan. Turn the oven off and allow the quiche to cool in the oven with the door slightly open for about 1 hour. Remove the quiche from the oven and allow it to cool completely before slicing.

You can reheat the quiche for about 15 minutes at 300°F (150°C) before serving. It can be stored covered in the refrigerator for up to 3 days.

*See photo on page 153.

NOTE

If you notice that the piecrust is getting too dark, place a piecrust shield on top or use a 10-inch (25-cm) piece of aluminum foil that you cut into a 9-inch (23-cm) circle from the center, leaving a foil ring you can place on top of the crust.

Everyday Artisan Bread

In long-ago England, the man who delivered food, loaves of bread, was called *hlaford* and his wife was *hlæfdige*, the loaf kneader. We know hlaford as lord and hlæfdige as lady.

It's with a good reason that the men and women who bake and supply us with bread would acquire such a prestigious social status. Bread is an everyday food we've become accustomed to and rely on. It's a symbol of prosperity and joy in many religions and holidays all around the world.

There are countless types of bread, bread recipes and bread-baking techniques. One can dedicate a lifetime to mastering and perfecting the art of bread baking.

But have no fear my dear friends, with the power of baking science and by using my foolproof formula, one can master the perfect loaf in a matter of one day.

Bread Ratio:
Flour 100%; Water 60%

Why do we need such a large amount of water?

Bread's biggest property is its elastic texture. Before being baked, it can be stretched and manipulated in many directions. Then when baked, it holds its shape very tightly and has a chewy, not so tender, bite.

Remember in Chapter 1 on page 17 when we discussed the properties of flour, we mentioned that the cause behind this elastic structure is the development of a gluten network.

For gluten to develop a strong, mature network, two things are needed: water and movement. There's a straight correlation between the amount of water we add and the strength of the gluten network. The more we add, the stronger the bond will be. Therefore, we need at least 60 percent liquid to form the ideal bread texture!

Baking a simple loaf of bread requires four ingredients: flour, water, yeast and salt.

Flour

Flour provides structure and stability to our breads and pastries. While the starches in the flour swell and thicken the dough, it's the gluten that's behind the elastic and chewy texture of bread and many other baked goods.

All-purpose or bread flour is a great option for making bread, but pastry flour and cake flour don't have a strong enough gluten network to carry the elastic structure of bread (see Cookie Butter Layer Cake recipe on page 19).

Water

Gluten is activated when mixed with water, so a large quantity of water is needed for the activation of the gluten molecules so they can bond with each other and create an elastic texture.

(continued)

EVERYDAY ARTISAN BREAD (cont.)

Yeast

Yeast is added to bread to ferment the dough and expand it as it releases gas. The fermentation process is long, but it's important and provides structure and flavor to the bread (see My Favorite Homemade Donuts recipe on page 80).

Salt

Salt, other than providing flavor to bread, actually helps strengthen the gluten bonds. The tightness of the bond is what helps create a starchy, elastic texture in bread and pastries, and salt helps tighten the bond.

How does the salt help?

Much like small batteries we buy, salt and flour also have positive and negative charges. Salt's structure is comprised of one positive sodium ion charge and one negative chloride ion charge. The gluten chains' structure is also made of positive and negative charges that by nature repel each other, at some parts, not allowing the gluten chain to get very close to each other.

Since negative neutralizes positive and positive neutralizes negative, when we then add the salt to the flour, its charges neutralize the gluten's charges. As a result, the gluten chains no longer carry any charges that repel each other and they can get closer together and form a tighter bond.

Mixing Method

When we mix bread dough, we need to make sure that we use the right temperature to activate the yeast and encourage fermentation.

Then, the water is added to the dry ingredients and yeast, which is when the gluten bonds will begin to activate. We make sure the gluten forms very strong bonds by kneading (mixing) our dough. Remember, longer mixing times create stronger gluten bonds.

Kneading times vary from recipe to recipe, but they usually take five to seven minutes on medium or medium-high speed if using a stand mixer or fifteen to twenty minutes if kneading by hand.

The dough is ready to rest and ferment once the gluten is developed, and that's easy to tell. The first sign is that the dough is fully hydrated and its surface is smooth. Another way to know is by taking a walnut-sized piece of dough and gently stretching it with our fingers. If the dough stretches into a paper-thin piece, then tears, it's ready. Don't expect it to keep stretching without tearing. If that happens, it's a sign that the dough was overworked and the bread will turn out too chewy.

You might notice that sometimes, when the dough is ready, it's smooth with a fully developed gluten but it still seems sticky. That's perfectly okay, and as the dough rests, the starches will continue to absorb the water, making the dough hydrated and ready to be divided and worked with.

Let's take a look at how I used the scientific techniques around gluten bonding to make the Chocolate Bread (page 159). This delicious bread has a crispy crust and a soft texture. You can use it to make sandwiches, toast it with some butter and you can even use it to make a delicious chocolate bread pudding. While this bread is loaded with delicious chocolate flavors, it is also a great option for both sweet and salty sandwiches.

The small amount of sugar in this recipe is added to activate the yeast and provide it food, not to sweeten it. (This bread isn't sweet.)

First, to speed up time, I decided to activate the yeast by mixing it with some sugar and half the amount of warm milk. But since the recipe uses instant dry yeast, you can skip this step and mix the yeast and sugar with the flour and add the milk with the second portion of milk.

Milk provides a lot of flavor, and since it's 90 percent water, it's also the source of liquid in this recipe. As you can read in the directions, the milk should be heated to 180°F (82°C), then cooled down to the right fermentation temperature. That's because milk contains glutathione, a substance that interferes with gluten formation and reduces the softness of the dough. Glutathione is destroyed by heat and heating the milk prior to using it in the recipe will help eliminate some of it.

Once the yeast has been activated, it's time to add the flour, cocoa, salt, remaining milk and butter, which will add some tender texture.

As the dough mixes, it might seem very dry and tough, but don't be tempted to add more water. There is just enough water to form elastic gluten chains. Adding more liquid might result in an over-developed gluten and a chewy texture to the bread.

Allow the dough to rest covered and in a warm spot. When it's time to roll and shape the dough, feel free to make rolls, add some chocolate chips or maybe even spread some chocolate filling. But honestly, this bread is best made into a Reuben sandwich!

CHOCOLATE BREAD

This recipe is a great example of the bread ratio and mixing method.

YIELD: One 8-inch (20-cm) loaf

1 cup (240 ml) milk, divided

2 tbsp (30 g) granulated sugar

1¼ tbsp (7 g) active dry yeast

2½ cups (350 g) bread flour

⅓ cup (29 g) cocoa powder

½ tsp salt

2 tbsp (28 g) unsalted butter, melted

Oil spray

Place the milk in a pan over the stove. Bring it to a boil, or until the temperature reaches 180°F (82°C). Remove from the heat and allow it to cool to 85 to 90°F (29 to 32°C).

In the bowl of a stand mixer, place ½ cup (120 ml) of the scalded and cooled milk, sugar, and yeast and use a fork to mix. Let sit for 20 to 30 minutes, until you notice thick foam at the top of the milk (that means that the yeast has been activated).

In a large bowl, sift together the flour, cocoa powder and salt.

Using the paddle attachment on low speed, sprinkle the flour mixture on top of the yeast mixture, followed by the remaining ½ cup (120 ml) of milk and butter.

Increase the mixer speed to medium. Once a shaggy mass has formed, replace the paddle attachment with the hook attachment and knead on medium speed for about 5 minutes, or until the bowl is clean and a smooth dough has formed. If the dough isn't coming together, add up to 2 tablespoons (30 ml) of warm milk (or water).

Spray the dough with some oil spray, then cover the bowl with plastic wrap and let it rise until doubled in size, 1½ to 2 hours. Once the dough has risen, grease a 3 x 8–inch (8 x 20–cm) loaf pan and place the dough on a clean work surface. Then, use your fist to gently punch the air out.

Using a rolling pin, roll the dough into a 3 x 12–inch (8 x 30–cm) piece, then roll it into a log starting from the side closest to you. Place the log in the prepared pan and cover it with a kitchen towel, or place it inside a plastic bag. Let it rise again until doubled in size, 2 to 3 hours.

When ready to bake, preheat the oven to 350°F (175°C) and bake on the middle rack for 45 to 50 minutes, or until the top is firm and the inside temperature is 190 to 200°F (88 to 93°C). Remove the loaf from the oven and allow it to cool for 5 to 10 minutes before removing it from the pan.

PUTTING IT ALL TOGETHER:
Use the Science You've Learned to Take Your Baking to the Next Level!

Congratulations! You did it, you baked your way through this book and now you can put your knowledge to use and bake some delicious treats using the science of baking. Please don't close the book if you have yet to do so. You can bake and enjoy these delicious recipes even if this is the first chapter you've flipped to.

This chapter includes some incredible recipes. The science is explained in each recipe, but unlike the previous chapters where we focused on one scientific principle, here each recipe demonstrates a few scientific principles and provides examples of how to incorporate a few principles in one recipe to create the best-ever version of whatever baked good you choose! If you find yourself in need of a memory refresher, you can always go back and reread a full description of the different scientific concepts.

The Perfect Cupcakes

We each have a different definition of the "perfect cupcake," but I have no doubt that once you bite into these amazingly delicious banana cupcakes (page 164), you'll nod your head and agree that these just might be THE BEST cupcakes.

Bananas and coffee are a match made in baking heaven. Each bite into these soft, tender and flavorful cupcakes is a melt-in-your-mouth symphony of deliciousness.

Throughout my baking journey, I've struggled with the idea of the perfect cupcake. I always imagined the perfect cupcake to be moist, rich and light. But not as rich as a pound cake or as light and airy as an angel food cake because in both cases, once the cupcake is frosted, it might be either too dense or not firm enough to hold the weight of the buttercream.

I kept those guidelines in mind when I contemplated this recipe. My intention was to create a light and moist cupcake with a firm structure that adds texture to the soft espresso meringue frosting.

Now that I had a clear vision of the texture, I decided to take the ingredient ratio of the Moist Quick Breads and Muffins formula (page 133) and the mixing method of the two-stages (page 116) formula and combine them to create my own new formula for the perfect cupcake.

The low percentage of fat in the muffin and quick bread ratio will prevent the cupcakes from separating from the liners. The large amount of liquid the ratio calls for will allow me to incorporate both a fresh banana for flavor and some sour cream that will balance the sweetness of the banana and sugar, as well as activate the baking soda and, as a result, add moisture and flavor to the mix (see the Nutty Bread recipe on page 72).

Lastly, it was time to decide which mixing method to use. The two-stages mixing method (see Rich Pound and Butter Cakes on page 116) where we aerate the dry ingredients then add the liquids, along with the extra step of folding meringue into the banana mixture, makes the cupcakes light, soft and tender with no resemblance to the dense texture of a muffin.

Truth to be told, while the smooth and soft meringue frosting goes wonderfully with the cupcakes, the cupcakes will stand up to the test of any type of frosting, including Old-Fashioned Buttercream (page 32), heavy whipping cream or even ganache (see page 148).

BANANA CUPCAKES WITH COFFEE FROSTING

This recipe uses the ingredient ratio of the Moist Quick Breads and Muffins formula (page 133), the two-stages mixing method (page 116), and the baking soda-acid reaction to create the best cupcakes.

YIELD: 15 cupcakes

CUPCAKES

1⅔ cups (199 g) cake flour

1½ tsp (7 g) baking powder

⅛ tsp baking soda

1 cup (200 g) granulated sugar, divided

1 medium (100 g) ripe banana

½ cup (120 ml) full-fat sour cream, room temperature

1 tsp vanilla extract

½ cup (114 g) unsalted butter, softened (cut into small cubes)

4 egg whites, room temperature

⅛ tsp cream of tartar

Preheat the oven to 350°F (175°C) and line 15 muffin cavities with cupcake liners. Set aside.

In the bowl of a stand mixer on medium-high speed, sift together the flour, baking powder and baking soda. Add ¾ cup (150 g) of sugar and use the paddle attachment to incorporate the ingredients.

In a medium bowl, mash the banana and mix it with the sour cream and vanilla.

Add the butter to the flour mixture and mix until the butter fully incorporates and the mixture resembles coarse sand. Pour in the banana mixture and blend until incorporated. The mixture should be thick and you might need to use a rubber spatula to fully incorporate the dry ingredients into the banana mixture. Set aside.

In a medium bowl, place the egg whites and cream of tartar, and using a hand mixer or a stand mixer, whisk on medium until frothy, 45 to 60 seconds.

Sprinkle in the remaining ¼ cup (50 g) of sugar and whisk until a soft meringue forms. Mix in about one-fourth of the meringue with the banana-flour mixture then fold in the remaining meringue.

Fill the cupcake liners three-quarters full and bake for 18 to 20 minutes. The cupcakes are ready when the tops appear matte (not shiny and wet) and a toothpick inserted into the center of the cupcakes comes out clean or with dry crumbs. Remove the cupcakes from the oven and allow them to cool before frosting.

FROSTING

1 tsp vanilla extract

2 tsp (7 g) instant coffee or espresso powder

1½ cups (300 g) granulated sugar, divided

¼ cup (60 ml) cup water

5 large egg whites

¼ tsp cream of tartar

To make the frosting, in a small bowl, pour the vanilla and sprinkle the instant coffee or espresso powder on top and allow it to dissolve.

In a medium saucepan, place 1¼ cups (250 g) of sugar and the water and swirl the pan to distribute the water. Place the pan on the stove over medium heat and cook until the sugar dissolves and the temperature reads 240°F (115°C), 4 to 5 minutes. (You'll need a candy thermometer.)

While the sugar cooks, place the egg whites and cream of tartar in the bowl of a stand mixer fitted with the whisk attachment and whisk until frothy. Sprinkle in the remaining ¼ cup (50 g) of sugar and whisk on medium.

When the sugar has reached 240°F (115°C), carefully pour it into the egg whites mixture while whisking. Increase the mixer speed to high and add the vanilla and coffee mixture.

Beat until a firm and stiff meringue forms, 3 to 4 minutes. (The bottom and sides of the mixer bowl should be cool to the touch of your hands.)

When ready, use a spoon to dollop some of the frosting on a cupcake, then torch the frosting with a kitchen torch if desired.

*See image on page 163.

The Ultimate Layer Cake

There is only one thing better than a handful of roasted pistachios and that's roasted pistachio cream cake. When baked into this creamy cake, the pistachio flavors evolve from delicious and nutty into rich and incredibly creamy.

There are a few steps and a lot of planning involved when making and assembling a layer cake. But the Pistachio Cream Layer Cake with White Chocolate Whipped Cream (page 168) is totally worth it.

The cake is light, tender, moist and full of creamy and nutty pistachio flavors. It's accompanied by a crunchy texture coming from the ground pistachios and a silky smooth texture coming from the white chocolate whipped cream.

When baking a layer cake, there are a few key elements we must keep in mind: flavors, texture and purpose.

The flavors should be recognized easily and complement the texture of the cake. For example, in this cake, to create a balance of both flavor and texture, some ground pistachios were added to the batter in addition to the pistachio paste.

Texture and purpose go hand in hand when it comes to layer cakes. The light and fluffy texture of a layer cake that's served at a casual afternoon picnic might be different than the texture of a rich and firm layer cake that's decorated and served at a wedding. There's no right or wrong, but each purpose requires different considerations and planning.

The pistachio cream cake is a great option for any occasion.

Since we want this cake to be strong enough to hold up the rich filling and another layer of cake, plus frosting, its structure should be firm enough to keep from falling apart, yet tender and light enough to eat without being too rich or dense. Therefore, using the butter cake ratio (page 116) is the perfect way to achieve a tender and soft cake with a sturdy structure.

The ingredients also have a big part in creating the tender and firm structure of the cake:

Flour

The low percentage of gluten in the cake flour will give the cake a soft and tender texture, while the all-purpose flour provides structure (see page 18).

Leaveners

The cake has 3 cups (366 g) of flour, which call for 3 teaspoons (11 g) of baking powder (1 teaspoon of baking powder per 1 cup [122 g] of flour; see page 75). In addition to 1 teaspoon of baking powder, ½ teaspoon of baking powder will replace 2 teaspoons (9 g) of baking soda that will be activated by the sour cream (page 71).

Fat

While the butter provides flavor, the vegetable oil adds tenderness and moisture to the cake. (See the Chocolate-Cherry Pop Tarts on page 49.)

Liquid

The sour cream activates the baking soda and, as a result, creates carbon dioxide gas that leavens the cake, salt that flavors the cake and water that adds moisture to the cake. (See the Nutty Bread recipe on page 72.)

The heavy cream provides flavor from the milk solids and fat. Notice that in this recipe we lightly whip the heavy cream, then fold it into the batter. This adds even more air into the batter and provides another layer of lightness and tenderness to the cake.

Eggs

The eggs emulsify the batter and they bond the fat with the liquids in the cake, all while providing structure that prevents the cake from collapsing (page 26). An addition of egg whites helps to further hold the structure of the cake.

Sugar and Pistachio Paste

The sugar sweetens the cake and provides moisture (page 58), and since it doesn't provide any flavor, the pistachio paste is added.

White Chocolate Whipped Cream

As mentioned on page 149, we need to use double and, sometimes, triple the amount of white chocolate when making white chocolate frosting. But in this recipe, we whip the cream and, as a result, thicken the ganache into a spreadable consistency that's stable enough for both filling and frosting the cake, so a smaller amount is required.

NOTE

While this frosting is great for filling and frosting, it's not stable enough for fondant-covered cake bases.

Simple Syrup

Sometimes layer cakes are filled, layered and stacked a few days before serving. The layers are soaked with simple syrup to add extra moisture to the cake and prevent it from drying out. (See the Maple Pecan Cake recipe on page 97.)

You can choose to skip it if you feel there's no need.

PISTACHIO CREAM LAYER CAKE WITH WHITE CHOCOLATE WHIPPED CREAM

This recipe is a great example of how balancing the stabilizing and tenderizing ingredients creates the ultimate layer cake structure and texture!

YIELD: One 8-inch (20-cm) cake

CAKE

1½ cups (180 g) cake flour

1½ cups (188 g) all-purpose flour

1 tsp baking powder

½ tsp baking soda

⅔ cup (66 g) finely ground toasted pistachios

¾ cup (180 ml) full-fat sour cream, room temperature

2 tsp (10 ml) vanilla extract

11 tbsp (154 g) unsalted butter, room temperature

1½ cups (300 g) granulated sugar

½ cup (120 ml) vegetable oil

½ cup (160 g) cream of pistachio (I used Vincente® Sicilian)

2 large eggs, room temperature

2 large egg whites, room temperature

½ cup (120 ml) heavy cream

To make the cake, preheat the oven to 325°F (160°C) and line the bottom of three 8-inch (20-cm) round pans with parchment paper. No need to grease the sides.

In a large bowl, sift together the flours, baking powder, baking soda and pistachios, then mix to blend and set aside.

In a large measuring cup, measure the sour cream and vanilla, mix to blend and set aside.

In the bowl of a stand mixer fitted with the paddle attachment, on medium speed beat the butter and sugar until fully blended, about 1 minute. Slowly drizzle in the oil, then increase mixer speed to medium-high and beat until light and fluffy, about 5 minutes. Make sure to scrape the bottom and sides of the bowl once or twice. Add the cream of pistachio and keep beating until fully incorporated, about 30 seconds.

Add the eggs and egg whites one at a time, waiting for each egg to fully incorporate before adding the next. Scrape the bottom and sides of the bowl, then reduce the speed to medium-low.

Add the flour mixture in three additions, alternating with the sour cream mixture, making sure to start and end with the flour mixture. Once you've added the last part of the flour, stop the mixer and finish blending using a rubber spatula, until all of the flour has been incorporated and the batter is cohesive and smooth.

In a separate clean bowl, whisk the cream (you can use a hand mixer) until soft peaks form, about 2 minutes, then gently fold the cream into the cake batter.

Divide the batter between the three prepared pans and bake for 35 to 40 minutes, or until a toothpick inserted into the centers of the cakes comes out clean. Remove the cakes from the oven and allow them to cool for about 10 minutes before removing them from the pans.

(continued)

PISTACHIO CREAM LAYER CAKE WITH WHITE CHOCOLATE WHIPPED CREAM (cont.)

SIMPLE SYRUP

1 cup (240 ml) heavy cream

½ cup (120 ml) water

1 cup (200 g) granulated sugar

FROSTING

2 cups (450 g) chopped white chocolate

2 cups (480 ml) heavy cream

6 tbsp (120 g) pistachio cream, for filling

½ cup (50 g) chopped roasted pistachios

NOTE

If you choose to decorate the cake with flowers, like I did, make sure to use edible flowers!

To assemble, make the simple syrup: In a medium saucepan over high heat, bring the cream, water and sugar to a boil. Reduce the heat to medium and cook the mixture for an additional 1 minute, or until the sugar has dissolved.

For easy filling and frosting, place the cakes in the refrigerator for about 30 minutes before layering and frosting.

The cake is best eaten at room temperature. Unfrosted, the cake can be stored at room temperature for up to 3 days or frozen for up to 1 month.

To make the frosting, place the white chocolate in a large bowl. Over the stove (or in a microwave), warm the cream over medium heat to just before it boils. This should take 4 to 5 minutes, but make sure to stay close. We don't want the cream to boil completely.

Pour the cream over the white chocolate and let it sit for 3 minutes. Use a hand whisk to melt the chocolate with the cream. Cover with plastic wrap and place it in the refrigerator until completely cool, about 3 hours or overnight.

Using a hand mixer, whisk the white chocolate–cream mixture until thick, about 2 minutes. Once it's thickened and you can see the strides of the whisk, stop mixing to prevent it from collapsing.

To assemble, place one layer of cake on top of your serving dish, level with a serrated knife if needed, then use a pastry brush to soak in ⅓ cup (80 ml) of the warm simple syrup. Allow it to soak in for 1 minute, then spread an even layer of pistachio cream, about 3 tablespoons (42 g), and a layer of white chocolate frosting, about ½ cup (132 g). Repeat with the second layer. Add the third layer, then use the remaining frosting to frost the top and sides of the cake then sprinkle with chopped pistachios.

The cake should be served at room temperature and refrigerated within 6 hours.

Crispy, Crumbly Cookies You'll Crave

I don't believe we should have to choose whether we're team "soft and chewy cookies" or team "crispy" cookies. We each have plenty of love to share among all cookies! Especially when it comes to anything s'mores flavored, so you can imagine what it's like to bite into crispy yet tender and crumbly S'mores Biscotti (page 173) that are gently dipped with chocolate and graham cracker crumbs and then generously loaded with a thick and fluffy homemade marshmallow. Yep, it's that good.

The key to creating a crispy cookie is to make sure that the amount of stabilizers in the recipe, such as the flour and eggs, is larger than the amount of tenderizers in the recipe, such as the fat, liquid and sugar.

In the biscotti recipe, the flour, cocoa powder and eggs are stabilizers, while the butter and sugar are tenderizers.

What makes these cookies crispy is, first, the fact that the amount of butter and fat is lower than the amount of flour and cocoa powder. Second, is the absence of moisture. Lastly, is the granulated sugar.

Now let's take a closer scientific look at the process:

About the fat: A smaller amount of butter means that there isn't enough fat to fully coat the flour and cocoa powder, resulting in a tougher bite (page 42). And although the small amount of butter isn't enough to fully coat and tenderize the flour and cocoa powder, it still provides a source of tender texture that prevents the cookies from being overly dry.

About the moisture: Stating that there isn't any moisture in the batter is scientifically not true, as there's some water in both the butter and the eggs. However, the large amount of starches coming from the flour and cocoa powder will absorb the liquids, leaving us with a dry and crumbly texture.

About the granulated sugar: Using granulated sugar with not enough moisture to turn it into an inverted sugar (page 58) is a great way to provide a brittle texture in a cookie since it will re-crystallize back into a crisp texture as the cookies cool.

Biscotti cookies are baked twice—once as a long log, then again after sliced as individual cookies. This method of baking the cookies twice is a great way to reduce the moisture in the cookies and make them crispy and brittle.

Once the cookies are baked, they're actually ready to be eaten and dipped into a large cup of milk. But to make them even better, we dip them with melted chocolate and thick and fluffy homemade marshmallow, then sprinkle them with graham cracker crumbs.

S'MORES BISCOTTI

This recipe is a great example of how we can manipulate the ratio of stabilizing and tenderizing ingredients to create the ideal biscotti texture!

YIELD: 30 cookies

BISCOTTI

2½ cups (300 g) all-purpose flour

⅔ cup (60 g) cocoa powder

1 tsp baking powder

½ tsp baking soda

½ salt

3 large eggs

1 tbsp vanilla extract

½ cup (114 g) unsalted butter, room temperature

1 cup (200 g) granulated sugar

DIPPING

1 cup (240 ml) melted chocolate chips

1 cup (102 g) graham crackers crumbs

To make the biscotti, preheat the oven to 350°F (175°C) and line one 13 x 18–inch (33 x 45–cm) pan with parchment paper. Set aside.

In a large bowl, sift the flour, cocoa powder, baking powder, baking soda and salt. Set aside.

Lightly beat the eggs and vanilla and set aside.

In the bowl of a stand mixer, beat the butter and granulated sugar on medium speed until fully combined, about 2 minutes. Scrape the bottom and sides of the bowl, then slowly drizzle in the beaten eggs. Beat until fully incorporated.

With the mixer on medium-low speed, add the flour mixture, then increase the speed to medium and beat until the dough comes together.

Divide the dough into two equal parts and shape each part into a 3 x 15–inch (7 x 38–cm) log. Bake for 30 minutes, then remove the pan from the oven and let it cool for 5 minutes. Reduce the heat to 300°F (150°C), and using a serrated knife, cut the logs into 1-inch (2.5-cm)-thick cookies, laying them flat on the side.

Bake for an additional 10 minutes, then turn the cookies to the other side and bake for an additional 10 minutes. Remove the cookies from the oven and let them cool completely before decorating.

To dip the cookies, start by placing the chocolate and graham cracker crumbs in two separated wide bowls. Dip the bottom of each cookie in the chocolate, shake to remove any excess chocolate, then dip them in the graham cracker crumbs. Place the cookies on a cooling rack sideways to cool.

(continued)

S'MORES BISCOTTI (cont.)

MARSHMALLOW

2 tsp (2 g) gelatin

1 tbsp (15 ml) water

4 large egg whites, from pasteurized eggs

½ tsp cream of tartar

½ cup (100 g) granulated sugar

To make the marshmallow, in a small bowl, place the gelatin and 1 tablespoon (15 ml) of water and mix to incorporate. Set aside and allow the gelatin to bloom.

In a bowl of a standing mixer, place the egg whites and cream of tartar then whip on high until a thick foam is formed. Gradually add the granulated sugar 1 tbsp (15 g) at a time counting 15 seconds before adding the next. Warm the gelatin in the microwave for 4 seconds, then with the mixer on medium-low speed, add it to the meringue, increasing the speed to high. Once a thick and sticky meringue is formed, turn the mixer off.

Dip or pipe each cookie in the marshmallow, and using a kitchen torch, toast the marshmallow.

Frosted cookies should be eaten the same day and unfrosted cookies should be stored at room temperature in an airtight container for up to 7 days.

NOTES

You can use store-bought marshmallow fluff instead of homemade marshmallow.

Do not use egg whites in a carton, they will not whip.

I recommend you wait about 5 to 7 minutes before dipping the cookies. The marshmallow takes 10 to 15 minutes to completely set.

Last-Minute Cake Made from Basic Pantry Items

I can't think of something more comforting than a slice of tender and moist cake exploding with chai spice flavors and topped with silky smooth cream cheese frosting. The beautiful combination of the moist cake with the smooth frosting, as well as the sweet and tangy flavors, make this cake the most delicious anytime-of-the-day treat.

If I tell you that making this incredible moist and tender Chai Cake with Cream Cheese Frosting (page 176) is not only easy and fast, but chances are you already have the ingredients in your pantry, would you believe me?

If you're like me, then more often than not you find yourself scratching your head because you were asked to contribute one of your delicious baked goods at the last minute, but there isn't enough time to better prepare and go shopping.

Well then, before you plan to head to the grocery store, I want you to take a look in your pantry. I promise that you have just what you need to bake the most delicious homemade cake, just like this delicious chai-spiced cake.

To bake a cake we need:

- Flour

- Sugar

- Eggs

- Liquids

- Leavening agents

- Fat

- Flavor

Since flour, leavening agents and eggs are part of the everyday pantry, let's focus on fat, flavoring and liquid.

When we're tight on time and waiting for the butter to soften isn't an option, we can always use melted butter or, even better, some vegetable oil (or any other oil), which will add moisture and tenderness to the cake. (See the Olive Oil Chocolate Pancakes recipe on page 53.)

Spices, extracts and juices are the best way to add flavor to any baked good. Maybe you even have some lemons at the bottom of the drawer in your fridge?

The type of sugar you use can also be a source of flavor. Light or dark brown sugar is coated with molasses and creates a rich flavorful syrup when baked (page 58). Honey or maple syrup is also a great option.

For liquid, you can literally use any source of liquid in your pantry or refrigerator, whether it's coffee, milk, juice, fruit puree, sour cream and, of course, water.

Let's take a closer look at the Chai Cake with Cream Cheese Frosting. The recipe calls for simple everyday ingredients like vegetable oil, applesauce, light brown sugar and spices.

The combination of these simple ingredients makes for an extraordinarily tender and moist cake. The vegetable oil tenderizes the cake, while the acidic applesauce provides even more moisture and flavor to the cake and the light brown sugar complements the spices that together bring extra flavoring to the cake.

You can even add some orange zest or nuts to turn this simple cake into a festive one.

CHAI CAKE WITH CREAM CHEESE FROSTING

This recipe is a great example of how we can balance the stabilizing and tenderizing ingredients to create an easy last-minute dessert.

YIELD: One 8-inch (20-cm) cake

CAKE

2 cups (250 g) all-purpose flour

1 tsp baking powder

½ tsp baking soda

1 tsp ground cinnamon

½ tsp ground ginger

¼ tsp ground cardamom

¼ tsp ground cloves

1 cup (240 ml) unsweetened applesauce, room temperature

1 tbsp (15 ml) vanilla extract

1 cup (220 g) dark brown sugar

2 large eggs, room temperature

1 large egg yolk, room temperature

1 cup (240 ml) vegetable oil

FROSTING

1 cup (232 g) full-fat cream cheese, room temperature

2 tbsp (28 g) unsalted butter, room temperature

1 cup (120 g) powdered sugar

1 tsp fresh orange zest

¼ cup (60 ml) heavy cream

NOTE

You can bake this cake using a 9-inch (23-cm) pan, just make sure to reduce the baking time by 7 minutes or so.

To make the cake, preheat the oven to 350°F (175°C), grease the bottom of one 8-inch (20-cm) round pan and line it with parchment paper. Set aside.

In a medium bowl, sift together the flour, baking powder, baking soda, cinnamon, ginger, cardamom and cloves. Set aside. In a separate bowl, measure the applesauce and vanilla. Set aside.

In the bowl of a stand mixer fitted with the paddle attachment, beat the brown sugar, eggs and egg yolk on medium speed until fully incorporated and the sugar is slightly lighter, 4 to 5 minutes. Slowly drizzle in the oil and beat until fully incorporated.

Add the flour mixture in three additions, alternating with the applesauce, making sure to start and end with the flour mixture.

Pour the batter into the prepared pan and bake for 40 to 45 minutes, or until a toothpick inserted into the center of the cake comes out clean. Remove the cake from the oven and allow it to cool in the pan for 10 minutes before removing. Frost the cake when it's cooled completely.

To make the frosting, in the bowl of a stand mixer fitted with the whisk attachment, beat the cream cheese and butter on medium speed until smooth, about 2 minutes. Gradually add the powdered sugar and mix until fully incorporated. Add the orange zest, then drizzle in the cream. Increase the mixer speed to medium-high and whip until fully incorporated and smooth with a spreadable consistency.

Using a spoon, frost the cake and serve at room temperature.

The cake should be refrigerated within 4 hours of frosting and can be stored for up to 3 days.

My Favorite Chocolate Chip Cookies

I believe a baker should be humble and never declare a chocolate chip cookie recipe as "the best," but that doesn't mean she cannot highly recommend a recipe to bake. Or the Brown Butter Chocolate Chip Cookies recipe (page 180) to be more exact.

These cookies are a little bit of everything and full of deliciousness. They're a bit chewy in the middle and a bit crunchy at the edges; they're soft enough to melt in your mouth but not so soft that they fall apart when you grab one.

There are no nuts, but there's a rich nutty flavor coming from the browned butter. Also, they're loaded with chocolate, but not in an overpowering way, more in a creamy, chocolaty way provided by the milk chocolate chips.

There are no secret ingredients or a new chemical reaction to learn in order to understand how to make these cookies so amazing. Simply applying the science of baking we covered throughout this book makes these cookies happen!

To give the cookies chewy centers and crispy edges, a combination of cake flour and bread flour is used (see page 18). While the protein in the bread flour will bond into strong gluten nets and provide a chewy bite to the cookies, the large amount of starches in the cake flour will balance out the tight protein bonds and provide the cookies with a tender, easy-to-bite texture. Later during baking, the water will easily evaporate from the starches at the edges of the cookies, which will create the crispy texture while the center remains hydrated and develops the chewy texture.

For a structure that's stable but still tender and soft, a combination of one egg and one egg yolk is added (page 26). The milk will add some moisture that will help the cookies spread.

The browned butter is added for its rich nutty flavor, and since the water in the butter has evaporated during the browning, it will provide tenderness to the cookies without strengthening the gluten development.

The light brown sugar also contributes deep flavors and some chewy texture, and since we also add granulated sugar, the cookies are not overly chewy and have a touch of crispiness.

There's no baking powder in the recipe. Baking powder will puff the cookies, giving them a cakey texture, while the baking soda will help to spread the cookies and allow the edges to get their crispy texture.

There's the same amount of milk chocolate chips as semisweet chocolate chips. The milk solids in the chocolate chips give the cookies an extra-creamy and sweet flavor.

BROWN BUTTER CHOCOLATE CHIP COOKIES

This recipe is a great example of how to select and utilize the properties of different stabilizing and tenderizing ingredients, as well as the Maillard reaction, to take favorite classics to the next level.

YIELD: 20 cookies

1 cup (227 g) unsalted butter

1½ cups (200 g) bread flour

1¼ cups (160 g) cake flour

1 tsp salt

1 tsp baking soda

1 large egg, room temperature

1 large egg yolk, room temperature

1 tbsp (15 ml) milk

1 tsp vanilla extract

1 cup (200 g) light brown sugar

¾ cup (150 g) granulated sugar

1 cup (168 g) milk chocolate chips

1 cup (168 g) semisweet chocolate chips

Preheat the oven to 350°F (175°C) and line two 13 x 18–inch (33 x 45–cm) cookie pans with parchment paper. Set aside.

Cut the butter into 1-inch (2.5-cm) pieces and place them in a medium saucepan over medium heat. Allow the butter to melt and keep cooking, about 5 minutes or until you no longer hear sizzling sounds and the butter changes its color to light brown and has a nutty smell to it.

Pour the browned butter into a large mixing bowl and allow it to cool while you prepare the rest of the ingredients.

In a large bowl, sift together the flours, salt and baking soda and mix to blend. Set aside.

In a medium bowl, mix together the egg, egg yolk, milk and vanilla. Set aside. Measure the sugars into the brown butter bowl, then add the egg mixture and stir to fully incorporate.

Add the flour mixture in three additions. There's no need to wait for the flour to fully incorporate before adding the next addition (this is just a step to make sure the flour will be fully blended and that there are no spills).

Fold in the chocolate chips and let the dough sit for 8 to 10 minutes to allow the flour to soak in the liquids. (Note that if the butter is too warm, it will melt the chocolate, so make sure the butter has cooled.)

Scoop the cookie dough using a medium cookie spoon (holds 1½ tablespoons), leaving 2½ inches (5 cm) of space between each cookie to allow spreading.

Bake on the middle rack for 8 to 10 minutes, remove from the oven and allow the cookies to cool for 5 to 10 minutes before moving them to a cooling rack. The cookies are ready when they have completely spread (no middle mound) and are lightly brown.

The cookies should be stored at room temperature in an airtight container for up to 3 days.

*See image on page 178.

Best Challahs Yet

This Timeless Traditional Challah (page 182) is a multi-purpose bread. It's a delicious, fluffy and tender challah you can rip with your hands and dip in your food. You can slice it and make a killer grilled cheese sandwich or, of course, French toast.

But the best most important part is that it's fun to work with and braid into the most beautiful and delicious challah that will wow your family and loved ones.

Growing up in a traditional Jewish home, my grandmother and mother both baked (my mom still does) fresh homemade challahs every Friday. Baking challah every week was more than just a delicious and fun tradition; it was, and still is, a way of giving thanks and appreciation to the opportunity of breaking bread.

Right before my mom and grandmother braided the challahs, they pinched a small piece of dough and set it aside as a reminder that some people don't have the same privilege. That recognition led to always baking more than needed and always setting an extra chair at the table in case someone hungry might knock at the door.

This strong bond with bread and its importance in our communities is what sparked my passion for baking and I couldn't think of a better way to close this book than dedicating it to my beloved mother, my grandmother Juliet and all of you home bakers.

Challah is a rich bread that's shaped into three-, four-, five- or six-braided loaves. Due to the kosher laws, challah gets its rich texture from eggs and egg yolks—never from butter or any other dairy products.

On page 155, I shared my bread formula and that its ratio calls for the amount of water to be 60 percent of the amount of flour to activate the gluten and form an elastic texture. But for this challah bread, we only use 1¼ cups (300 ml) of water, which is even less than 40 percent of the amount of flour.

There are a few reasons for that. The first is that the eggs and egg yolks also contain water (remember from the stabilizers section on page 26) that contributes to the formation of strong gluten bonds. The sugar in this challah is a hygroscopic substance (see the Browned Butter–Coffee Blondies recipe on page 63), which absorbs water from its surroundings as well. In this case, the sugar absorbs the moisture coming from the air we incorporate into the dough during the long mixing process.

Another reason is to help the challah maintain its shape and strand definition, so we can see the braiding. When we add too much water, the dough turns out dense, heavy and sometimes too sticky to roll and braid. During the second rising time, the heavy dough tends to spread flat in the pan and lose its shape, while the strands blend with each other and our eyes cannot recognize the separation.

In this recipe, the combination of flours will allow an elastic dough to develop that doesn't stick when rolled and braided but has a soft texture.

While egg yolks can add a much richer texture than whole eggs, it's important to use both whole eggs and egg yolks. The egg yolks for rich texture (as well as the olive oil) and whole eggs increase the number of proteins that will set the dough and help the challah maintain its shape during baking.

The recipe calls to divide the dough and shape it into braided loaves; however, you can shape it in any way you choose.

TIMELESS TRADITIONAL CHALLAH

This recipe is a great example of combining the right balance of stabilizing and tenderizing ingredients, then using the bread ratio and mixing method.

YIELD: Two 1-pound (454-g) loaves

3¼ cups (406 g) all-purpose flour

3 cups (400 g) bread flour

⅓ cup (66 g) granulated sugar

1 tbsp (12 g) active dry yeast

2 tsp (12 g) salt

1 large egg

5 large egg yolks

¼ cup (60 ml) olive oil

1–1¼ cups (240–300 ml) warm water (90°F [32°C])

1 large beaten egg, to brush the challah

¼ cup (36 g) sesame, poppy, pumpkin or sunflower seeds

In the bowl of a stand mixer, sift the flours, sugar, yeast and salt. On low speed, use the paddle attachment to mix the ingredients for 1 minute.

In a medium bowl, mix together the egg, egg yolks and oil. Drizzle in 1 cup (240 ml) of warm water into the egg mixture and mix to incorporate.

With the mixer on low speed, drizzle the wet ingredients into the dry mixture. Once a shaggy mass forms, replace the paddle attachment with the hook attachment and knead on medium speed for 8 to 10 minutes, until the dough is smooth. If after about 45 seconds of mixing you notice that there's still some flour that doesn't incorporate into the dough, add 1 tablespoon (15 ml) of lukewarm water (up to 4 tablespoons [60 ml]).

Lightly oil a large bowl (oil spray is okay), place the dough in the bowl and lightly oil the dough. Cover the bowl with a plastic bag, place it in a warm spot in your kitchen and let it rest for 3 to 4 hours or until doubled in size.

Line two 13 x 18–inch (33 x 45–cm) pans with parchment paper. Set aside.

Punch the dough down once and place it on a clean work surface, then divide the dough into 12 evenly sized pieces (each about 4 ounces [100 g]). Each piece should be about the size of a baseball. Roll each piece into a 14-inch (35-cm) log and braid two six-braided loaves, three four-braided loaves or four three-braided loaves. Place each challah in the prepared pans, brush with the beaten egg and sprinkle with your choice of seeds.

Allow the challahs to rest and rise for 3 to 4 hours, or until doubled in size.

Preheat the oven to 350°F (175°C) and bake for 25 to 30 minutes, or until the inner temperature reaches 190 to 200°F (88 to 93°C)

Remove the challahs from the oven and immediately place them on cooling racks.

The challahs are best eaten within 1 day and can be wrapped in aluminum foil and frozen for up to 3 weeks.

Resources

How Baking Works: Exploring the Fundamentals of Baking Science, Third Edition, by Paula Figoni

On Food and Cooking: The Science and Lore of the Kitchen by Harold McGee

Ratio: The Simple Codes Behind the Craft of Everyday Cooking by Michael Ruhlman

Science and Cooking: Physics Meets Food, From Homemade to Haute Cuisine by Michael Brenner, Pia Sörensen and David Weitz

Science & Cooking: From Haute Cuisine to Soft Matter Science by Harvard EDX (edx.org)

The Pie and Pastry Bible by Rose Levy Beranbaum

Acknowledgments

I would first like to thank the wonderful, passionate and creative community of bakers, readers and followers out there who supported my work, baked my recipes and always had kind words to share and encourage me with. As well as the wonderful bakers, Rose Levy Beranbaum, Joanne Chang, Dorie Greenspan, Jenny McCoy, Michelle Lettrich and so many more who shared their knowledge throughout the years and help keep the flame alive.

For my food-photography teachers and mentors, Sarah Crawford, Jenn Davis, Rachel Korinek, Joanie Simon and Kimberly Espinel. This book would not have happened without the sharing of your knowledge, expertise and passion.

A big thank you to the amazing team at Page Street Publishing for giving me this amazing opportunity to further explore, experiment and bring this book to life. Thank you for your patience and for encouraging me throughout this process.

Thank you to my loving and supportive husband who always believed in me and never had a doubt this book could come to life. To my beautiful daughters, Emily and Juliet, your smiles and hugs are what all this is for.

Thank you to the wonderful women in my life, my mother-in-law Regina, my dear friends Dae, Jenni, Brie and Eleanor whose support and kind words were always the biggest motivation.

And the biggest thank you to my parents, David and Rutty Levy, who taught me to always be true to myself and my beliefs, for teaching me the values of hard work, honesty and kindness. And to always dream.

About the Author

Dikla Levy Frances is a self-taught baker and baking scientist. She was born and raised in Israel and moved to the United States in 2008, and she is greatly influenced by her Moroccan and Iranian culinary roots.

Her passion for baking and the science behind it was the reason she founded the sweet baking blog One Sarcastic Baker, where she shares recipes and tips for better baking as well as beautiful photography. Dee's work has been featured on feedfeed, Wilton.com and The Nosher.

Index